ELLIE EDWARDS - NOLAN SAN

SAVE YOUR MARRIAGE

A COUPLE'S WORKBOOK

HOW TO FACE AND SOLVE 18 KEY ISSUES OF YOUR LIFE AS A COUPLE:
STOP FIGHTING AND LIVE A FULFILLING RELATIONSHIP OF LOVE AND FAITH

INCLUDES 52 WEEKLY DEVOTIONS FOR COUPLES

2 BOOKS IN 1

TIME TO TALK ABOUT US
MARRIAGE COUNSELING FOR COUPLES

18 steps to a solid and happy marriage with guided conversations.
A modern workbook based on the experience of hundreds of real
couples

A COUPLE'S DEVOTIONAL
OUR JOURNEY WITH GOD

A year of devotions for married couples.
52 weekly scripture-based reflections to nurture
your relationship and grow together in faith.

TABLE OF CONTENTS

BOOK 1 – TIME TO TALK ABOUT US

Introduction 8

Step 1 - Getting To Know Each Other 12

Step 2 - Drawing A Path Together: Your Expectations, Mutual Trust, Your Strengths, And Your Commitment As A Couple 20

Step 3 - Creating Moments Of Sharing: Daily Activities, Couple Rituals, Future Projects, Smiling And Having Fun Together 23

Step 4 - Learn To Communicate And Listen To Each Other All The Time: Not Only Love But Complicity 29

Step 5 - Intimacy And Sex: Opening Up Without Shame And Keeping Desire Alive 33

Step 6 - Children: How To Become Parents Together 41

Step 7 - Work And Finances: Respect Each Other's Work Needs And Find A Fair Compromise, Deciding Together How To Invest Your Money 50

Step 8 - How To Face And Solve Conflicts 56

Step 9 - Everyday Life And The Power Of Small Gestures .. 65

Step 10 - Spiritual Life And Gratitude 73

Step 11 - Become An Expert About Your Partner 78

Step 12 - Common Relationship Mistakes And Making Marriage A Success 85

Step 13 - Ways To Build Emotional Intimacy With Your Partner 92

Step 14 - Spice Up Your Sex Life.................................100

Step 15 - Analyzing And Attacking Anxiety.....................109

Step 16 - Keep your Personal Space and Love Yourself.....116

Step 17 - The Importance of being able to Manage Family 122

Step 18 - No More Fighting......................................143

Conclusion 151

BOOK 2 - A COUPLE'S DEVOTIONAL

Introduction..161

Week 1: Know Each Other 164

Week 2: Respect Each Other.................................171

Week 3: Flexibility 172

Week 4: Confidence 175

Week 5: Emotional Needs and Resources.....................178

Week 6: Spirituality...181

Week 7: Intimacy 187

Week 8: Learn To Communicate Always 192

Week 9: Resolve Conflicts 198

Week 10: The Small Stuff....................................201

Week 11: To Grow the Relationship..........................204

Week 12: To Forgive...205

Week 13: Always Help Each Other In Difficulties..........207

Week 14: Always Keep the Relationship Lively 209

Week 15: Smile and Play Together 212

Week 16: Gratitude 214

Week 17: Give And Receive Love 214

Week 18: Financial Planning And Decision-Making: What Are Your Habits? 215

Week 19: Listen To One Another 217

Week 20: The Spice of Appreciation 219

Week 21: Steer Clear Of the Desires of the Body 221

Week 22: Reconciliation over Retaliation 222

Week 23: Protect the Sanctity of Marriage 223

Week 24: Affirmation That Strengthens 226

Week 25: Learning Each Other's Language 227

Week 26: The Comparison Trap 229

Week 27: Open And Honest Discussions 231

Week 28: Sacred Roles to Play 234

Week 29: Handling Frustration in Marriage 236

Week 30: Build Your Marriage on the Positives 238

Week 31: Marriage Is Holy, Treat It As Such 242

Week 32: Intellectual 243

Week 33: Interdependence 244

Week 34: Don't Compete, Coordinate 245

Week 35: Creating Habits 248

Week 36: Parenting Together 248

Week 37: Loving Without Limits 250

Week 38: Spend Some Time Together 251

Week 39: Remember Holiness and Purity 252

Week 40: Laying the Perfect Foundation 253

Week 41: True Generosity 255

Week 42: Think Before You Respond 256

Week 43: Keep your Word 258

Week 44: Anxiety in Relationship 260

Week 45: Confidentiality 262

Week 46: God Should Be the Center 264

Week 47: Equality over Inequality 265

Week 48: Set Relationship Goals 266

Week 49: Money and Finances 268

Week 50: Physical Intimacy 269

Week 51: Alone Time Matters 272

Week 52: God Is Always With Us 273

Conclusion 276

Let's be real. Lots of people struggle in their marriages. Just consider that the divorce rate is 50% for first marriages and much higher for second or third marriages. That alone is a lot of people who struggle enough to call it quits. But that does not account for all the people who stay married but are miserable, frustrated, feeling empty, and stuck. They don't know how to stay and make it better, but they also don't know how to leave the relationship either. So, they remain unhappy and paralyzed with indecision. They complain to their girlfriends about their husbands, maybe drinking too much wine, spending too much money, or spending far too much time distracting themselves with flirtations on social media, so they don't have to think about the fact that they are both unhappy and stuck. They numb themselves, so they don't ever have to face the reality of their lives head-on. So, of course, nothing ever really changes one way or the other. The relationship never feels good, but at the same time, they do not leave for something else that would make them feel better. Here's why:

We tell ourselves that we've tried everything we can to make the relationship better and nothing has worked. But you would probably also agree with me that we've had zero training and have not been equipped with the tools to be successful. Let's say we set out to write a workbook and thought to ourselves, "It should be easy enough. Just type in about 50,000 words into a computer. How difficult can that be?" That's the equivalent of what we do when we enter into a long-term relationship. We think to ourselves, "We love each other. We said we would stay together forever. How difficult can it be?"

We both know there's so much more to writing a workbook than just finding 50,000 random words and typing them into Microsoft Word. You have to know who you're speaking to and what their problem is (in their specific words). You have to have an outline and path through the pain to be able to help them with their problem. Otherwise, you're wasting their time, and they won't get past page three. You have to be clear about how you want them to be different by the end of the workbook. Oh, and then, you have to know how to get it published, and into the hands of the people who have the problem, you help solve. Easy enough, right? (Did you know 90% of people say they want to write a workbook, but most never do?)

Likewise, being in relationship with the same person is not for the faint of heart. And we've gone into this without any training, tools, or even role-models to help do this well – particularly when things get complicated. In our opinion, this is like asking someone to write a workbook in English who barely speaks the language. It's going to be painful for the author – and the reader.

I know for sure that, at this point, you haven't tried everything. You might have tried everything you know, but what about all the tools that you don't know? What about the concepts that have worked for thousands of people, but sadly, no one taught you how to implement? You may have tried what you know, but most of us know precious little about how to create and sustain a relationship throughout a lifetime.

Failing in Advance: Sometimes, people have given up before they even start. They determine upfront that it's not going to work, and they tell themselves, "I've heard it all before, my relationship is different. This won't work for us." Unfortunately, these people won't ever really try to solve their problem. They will tell themselves they're trying because they're buying workbooks and courses and reading every online article they can find, but they're not doing what's required to solve the problem. Instead, they choose not ever to try so they won't ever fail...which is just a way of failing in advance.

The purpose of the workbook is to be a guide for married couples or couples who are about to get married, to have a happy and lasting married life together.

We are a married couple for more than twenty years. We are already in the 40s. 45 years old and 48 years old to be exact. We have studied couple therapy and psychology for years. We have helped many couples of friends and relatives over the years to find the right way to a long and peaceful couple's life.

This workbook comes from the real everyday experiences of all of them.

Enjoy it and never stop growing together!

The more you know and are willing to learn about your partner, the closer you will become and at a much faster pace. Finding a few bits of information to identify with will help offer you the reassurance that you've found your forever mate. You don't want to be identical twins about everything, but a few things in common gives you an instant bond. Some areas such as goals and values are essential to be on the same page for relationship success.

Know the History of Your Partner

Knowing a few of the basics in the history of your partner and openly sharing your history will give each of you a foundation to begin exploring more in-depth. You can't be expected to remember everything in the beginning but build on information as time goes by. A few of the things to start with could be:

- Where they were born.

- Where they grew up.

- The size of their family.

- Where their family is located.

- Education level.

- Profession and job experiences.

- Any past serious relationships/marriages.

- Any children and where they are located.

A small amount of information to start will allow you to initiate conversations that lead you to learn even more. It's essential to have enough information to feel comfortable that you are making a great choice in partners.

<u>Discuss Life Ambitions and Goals</u>

What are your goals in life? Are you wanting to live in a big city or have dreams of a small cottage near the woods? Do you like fancy cars, or is an old 4X4 pickup all you'll ever want and need? What are your ambitions with career, homeownership, salary, retirement plans, and savings? You can find out the same information in return. It's vital to ensure you and your partner have ambitions and goals that line up with one another or you will end up a miserable person.

<u>Know their Core Values and Whether they Line up with Your Own</u>

Core values are the value you place on things like honesty, integrity, work ethic, compassion, and more. It would be difficult to establish a long-term relationship with someone that did a little shoplifting or found lying to be no big deal if those are not your values as well. It's a recipe for immediate disaster. Most core values are established before the age of six, although it doesn't mean that values can't be added to and expanded throughout your life. It's good to know where you're starting and see where things align and where there are potential problems.

What are their Tastes in Music, Movies, Books, Food?

Great conversations require a good supply of basic interests and knowing what their tastes are in music, movies, books, food, fashion, and all things current or trendy. The better you share the intricate likes and dislikes of basics in life, the wider the arena is for powerful conversations. It's also nice to know areas you may differ, at least slightly. It can help expose you to something different you might end up loving just as much. Every person that loves Mexican food never realized it until giving it a try. Sharing new experiences forces you to look at your favorites in a new light. It can breathe new life into what had become stagnant.

What is their Favorite Color, Animal, Car, and More?

Keep it going! You aren't finished in the learning process if you are going to become a real expert in your partner. You still need to discover essential things like what is their favorite color, favorite car, favorite animal, and whether they prefer gold or silver. It's almost as if a floodgate opens and the conversations become powerful and filled with vital information. It also provides plenty of clues on what you can get for birthdays, holidays, and anniversaries. The sky is the limit in asking the question but try and spread out the questioning over a long period.

Are they a Deep Thinker or Impulsive by Nature?

How a person communicates can have a lot to do with their baseline personality. You'll be able to make observations as easily as they can see where you sit on the spectrum. More reserved, deep-thinking individuals often seem to have fewer words to say. They tend to place a lot of emphasis on the words used, however. It could be that they are introverted. It doesn't mean they are shy but more deliberate and selective in action.

A more impulsive person is generally considered an extrovert. Although it may appear to be all over the map, the tasks and conversations are skillful and done in their special way. You'll find that the more impulsive personalities hardly ever run out of conversational topics. Most are upbeat and highly energetic. Making these simple observations can point you in the best directions for starting and continuing a conversation.

What are Some of their Basic Habits?

Learning a few of their basic habits will help make you an expert on your partner. Do they go jogging every Monday and Wednesday morning? Is there a show they have to watch on Friday evenings? Do they prefer to drink coffee out on the patio on their day off? Do they have an irritating twitch to their eye if you leave a dirty dish in the sink after a midnight snack? Studying and understanding the habits of your partner will help you work more in unison and help create a happy home environment.

What do they need from a Relationship?

All parts of information you gather culminate in showing you what they are looking for and need from a relationship. Ask the important questions, assimilate the information, and use it to help create a smoother transition into the relationship.

Learning about your partner should be something you look forward daily. Most successful relationships are not based on a perfect fit. It's finding ways to fit together in the uneven areas that make the difference. Finding ways to grow together is the ultimate goal.

Know What's in Their Suitcase

Every person carries a suitcase of beliefs and ideals that shape the everyday view and perception of the world. Most are not comfortable with showing this to people they are not familiar and comfortable with, including you, initially. Begin unpacking this suitcase and taking a look at the contents at your first opportunity. You must be willing to allow them access to your suitcase. Being open and honest in communication is critical to growing together instead of apart.

The Importance of Seeing the Complete Package

The process of unpacking this suitcase and giving each area an inspection begins during the dating phase. It's good to explore what your partner's beliefs are in every aspect of life, love, and human interaction. How well will they get along with people, even beyond their relationship with you? Are they able to hold a steady job and relate well to friends? Are they frequently bumping heads with authority figures? Do they seem mature when it's required? It's important to look at these details to understand the big picture fully. The way they communicate or fail to communicate with others can be a warning sign that things can break down.

Are You Seeing Stable Moods and a Compatible Personality?

Sudden and drastic mood swings in a partner can make life miserable. Do they seem to have a stable countenance most of the time? Women can get thrown off by monthly hormonal changes, but it can also indicate their ability to handle stress and anxiety. Talking about possible stressors and ways to reduce anxiety can help you and your partner. As long as your basic personalities seem compatible, the rest is workable. Your partner will be in awe that you are willing to help them talk through their worries and anxieties.

What Makes Your Partner Emotional?

All people have a different threshold of emotional response to everything in life. Emotional control and the ability to show emotion are equally important in being able to convey feelings properly. Do they have problems discussing emotional subjects? Do you have to be the one to initiate affection? It's important to find a happy medium that allows both of you to feel comfortable sharing and demonstrating emotional responses. It may be that your partner needs to venture out of their comfort zone and experience a new way of responding to things.

What are their Pet Peeves?

Pet peeves are little things that drive people bonkers! It's handy to know what these things are with your partner. You should also relay any of your pet peeves to them. It could something as slight as not loading the dishwasher the way they normally do the job. Learning what the pet peeves are for each of you and avoiding them will help bring a more harmonious atmosphere to the home. Instead of viewing them as a bit of trivial information, think about how you feel when your pet peeve is right in front of you. Shoes left in the middle of the floor, laundry piled in a corner instead of the hamper, or whatever really makes your blood boil.

What are their World Views?

How does your partner view the world? Are there any strong political views that might clash with your own? Are fears of a tanking world economy one of the first things they talk about every morning? The last thing anyone wants first thing in the morning is to hear political ranting and raving. It's worth exploring what their world views are and how you can help minimize any conflict by avoiding particular topics of discussion. It's not the end of the world to hold differing views.

Why Do they Hold their Particular Views?

If your partner holds strong world views and seems majorly opinionated, try and find out why they feel the way they do. It's often a generational idea passed down through families. Are they okay with your views being a little different or less strong? The last thing you want is to feel you have to convert to any beliefs and views you are not comfortable with, any more than they would want to convert to yours. Most people tend to fall somewhere in the moderate range of political and world views. It's rarely a big problem in most relationships.

Is There Any Extra Baggage?

People tend to carry extra baggage with them you can't always detect immediately. It could be old hurts carried over from a disastrous relationship or marriage. It might be from suffering abuse as a child. Incidences like this that leave pain and trauma can affect how they respond and deal with people. It can lead to problems with trust or fears of abandonment. You need to listen for a few keywords when all of these various topics are discussed. Some words to look for are:

- Divorce – parental or their own.

- Child custody problems.

- Child abuse.

- Spousal or partner abuse.

- Alcoholic or drug addict upbringing.

- Cheating partner.

How to Become an Expert Baggage Handler

The fact that someone is carrying a little extra baggage doesn't make them a bad potential partner. It might take time and patience to win over their trust completely. Your partner might automatically begin to feel high levels of anxiety if you don't make it home right when expected and rush to think you're cheating. Keep your cell phone handy and call if you are running late. A little gesture like this will help put their mind at ease and keep them out of an older, bad place.

Step 2 - DRAWING A PATH TOGETHER: YOUR EXPECTATIONS, MUTUAL TRUST, YOUR STRENGTHS, AND YOUR COMMITMENT AS A COUPLE

Identifying Your Strengths and Problem Areas

The point of contact easily disappears from view in conflict situations. Situations become exaggerated when each person tries to convince or weaken. It is not surprising that people ignore areas of mutual interest, lose the ability to recognize, learn and rely on what they already have in common.

Create a common interest in marriage

By accepting someone you disagree with, you may feel that you are losing ground. But a study found that effective negotiators turn to areas of agreement three times more often than inactive negotiators. The point of contact is important for resolving a conflict because it is often forgotten or uncared for. If nobody is looking for a common language, how will it be built?

Remember the conflict situation in your life when you and the other person wanted to understand it, but it got worse. Are you thinking about where the common thing was between you?

Types of common interests in marriage

Even in the most difficult conflict situations, you can take on many common basic factors that are simply based on our

20

common humanity. The general point is that both people can be understood and want to find a solution. Everyone may also find it difficult to find their true message. There is a general weakness in emotional stress and pressure, although this will be tested differently. Despite the tension that can arise in a conflict, there is usually one common factor: don't try to hurt anyone.

Tips for creating a common interest in marriage

Listen and recognize another point of view: you can also thank someone for listening to you. Remember that even when you are different, understanding is an important starting point. Customize the discussion by expression when the discussion is not easy and you want the discussion to go well despite the pressure. Pay attention and recognize the steps of the discussion - small and large. Refer to areas of agreement when discussing other problems.

Define common goals. When you turn your attention to the issues discussed, it is often easy to find that there are common goals, despite the differences in how they are achieved.

Lessons of general interest in marriage

The prospect of common interests encourages us to go beyond the desire to "prove our point of view", "be right" or another severe judge. Common ground helps to understand and accept a complex situation. It helps us to focus on our behavior, as well as on the behavior of others.

If you consider common ground, this can be a useful guide to get back on it if the negotiations are at a dead end. Also, a common interest is a basis that needs to be expanded so that the areas of the agreement become larger and larger.

People tend to react the same way to situations until the pattern is broken. It is enough for a person to start highlighting common ground, so his negotiating partner will be more willing to do the same. You still don't agree, everything is in order - the key is that a common language provides an antidote to the models that contribute to conflict and create distance.

Common interests easily disappear from sight in conflict situations. Situations become exaggerated when each person tries to convince or weaken. It is not surprising that people ignore areas of mutual interest, lose the ability to recognize, learn and rely on what they already have in common.

Step 3 - CREATING MOMENTS OF SHARING: DAILY ACTIVITIES, COUPLE RITUALS, FUTURE PROJECTS, SMILING AND HAVING FUN TOGETHER

Everyone brings a semblance of ritual and tradition into a relationship. The problem is, there's never any room for two, and rarely are two people raised from the same situation and circumstance. You might have been married before and have certain ritual ways you celebrate anniversaries or holidays. Your partner might have grown up as an only child and is not used to sharing space. Coming from different worlds can cause friction, or it can be viewed as a great starting point for a new life.

<u>The Blending of Two Worlds</u>

A serious relationship that leads to marriage will mean blending all of your individual family rituals, traditions, beliefs, and values. It's often easier to let many of them go and simply start from scratch. The reasons you carefully consider the values and beliefs of the other person when embarking on a relationship path become painfully clear at this point. When base-line values, goals, and beliefs are too off, the relationship will struggle. It's commonly referred to as being unevenly yoked and can spell disaster for the future plans of the relationship.

It doesn't mean that the mountains are impassable. All you have to do is look for the right valleys and paths to make your way over, around, and through them. Every serious relationship has had to deal with these issues, but many didn't give it much thought beforehand. It's hard to see the possible warning signs of future conflict when everything seems to be fun, new, and exciting. Eventually, the reality of the situation sets in and you learn that forming your rituals and traditions is usually the easier path.

The Importance of Rituals and Traditions

Rituals and traditions rule your life more than you might think of at the moment. It amounts to almost every repeated action we take, whether it's holiday times, special days, or an everyday meal. Let explore what some of these are, so you can have a better picture of what you will have to deal with when blending lives.

What are Rituals?

Rituals are actions you take regularly, usually on a daily or weekly basis. Some of these are lifelong and hard to break. A few examples of rituals are:

- Sitting down at the table for meals or eating in front of the television.

- Daily exercise routine.

- Jogging or walking each day.

- Certain days for chores like laundry or vacuuming.

What are Traditions?

Traditions are things you do, places you go, and specialty items you eat or drink for special occasions. Holidays are normally filled with traditions.

A few examples are:

- New Year's Eve and Champagne.

- Birthday dinner out.

- Thanksgiving meal prep at home or with family.

- Valentine's Day expectations.

- Christmas gift opening.

All individual rituals and traditions will have to be explored to see if you have some common ground. Many times, the traditions and rituals must be replaced for ones that work best for both of you.

Holidays, Birthdays and Anniversaries

Unless you are a couple that doesn't care to celebrate any holidays, anniversaries, or birthdays, you will have to do some work to try and blend the traditions that are favorable to both of you. Each will come with their own experiences and family traditions and the results will be something new that is either a hybrid of both or a completely new creation.

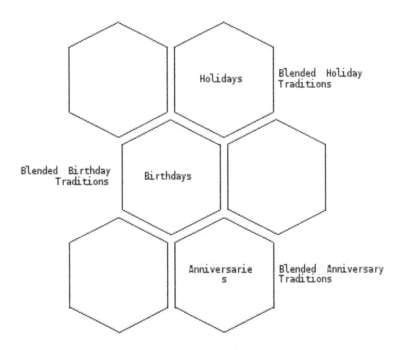

Holidays

Blended Holiday Traditions

Blended Birthday Traditions

Birthdays

Anniversaries

Blended Anniversary Traditions

Blending traditions

One example of blending traditions is when you enjoy cooking a nice birthday meal, but your partner cannot cook. You can always blend the traditions. You cook their birthday meal and they take you out to a restaurant for yours. It's the perfect blend and solution.

Creating Memories and Standards

The important part of coming together as a couple is to communicate about what is enjoyable to you about certain rituals and traditions. No matter how you decide to proceed as a couple, make great memories and set the standards you want for your own new family. You can completely veer from all the rituals and traditions you know and establish new ones.

Create More than You Borrow

A fun and enjoyable part of becoming a solid couple is to establish new traditions and rituals that are distinctly your own. Borrowing the parts that are an important part of your past and incorporating them can be done, but make sure you discuss everything to the point of being comfortable with any decisions. Create new rituals and traditions based on the things you love to do and are important as a couple. Where will your new combined interests take you? Maybe you will begin taking summer vacations and make that a tradition. Perhaps it will be sitting at a favorite café on the weekends drinking a latte. It's all up to you and your partner.

Appreciate the New Traditions and Rituals

Enjoy and appreciate all of the new traditions and rituals, as well as any blended ones you design for your joint lives. Your life together will continue to evolve, and the daily communication practiced will help you change things up as you see fit. You might have to continue with some rituals and traditions on your own. It's fine as long as you develop a healthy number of ones you can enjoy together.

Step 4 - LEARN TO COMMUNICATE AND LISTEN TO EACH OTHER ALL THE TIME: NOT ONLY LOVE BUT COMPLICITY

I hope the two of you bring up "I" statements, non-verbal communication, and dialectical behavior therapy. As you know, this route of therapy in psychology has several attributes, but the main one is the idea of confronting one issue at a time instead of being overwhelmed by all of the potential issues that could come up. With these three communication skills under your belt, you will be well-prepared for dealing with any problems in communication that may come your way.

I want to add another communication skill that you should add to your list of skills in communication that you need to learn, and that is active listening.

You can get so much more out of communication with your spouse when you are an active listener. It means you don't just make them believe you are listening so they will listen to you better, but you actually do listen to them.

This sincerely benefits you in the end, since it helps you gain valuable information. It tells you what is on their mind, which can only help you in your relationship. Maybe you don't always make as much effort as you should to get into your significant other's mind, but it is truly worth the small hassle.

You are sure to have noticed examples of effective communication between couples in your daily life. Discuss healthy, conscious couples you know and find conflict resolution strategies that you both like.

Before, you did a similar activity, but it was in the context of what makes a marriage work. This time, I want your focus to be on only the role of communication in a conscious married relationship. Not only that, but I want you to ask yourselves what specific communication skills you think will be the most helpful to you in your specific problems.

For example, if one or both of you are always saying you aren't listened to, both of you should put some effort into honing your active listening. I say both of you should do it because this is how any self-improvement you make in dialectical behavior therapy should be. You may have an idea of who is mostly responsible in your head, but both of you should do it anyway.

For one thing, when both spouses do the same self-improvement practices, we sidestep the problem of blame that we are always trying to avoid in this kind of therapy. For another, you will still get value out of it even if you don't think you need it. People who are better at active listening than your average person can still improve; people who can control the tone of their voice very well can still learn how to do it better.

This is an important thing to do because while this workbook can give you tools to tackle any situation in your marriage, applying these tools to your real life will be more practical if you can see them in action.

So far, you have gotten relatively deep into communication topics, and you have done some of the exercises in the workbook, but most of your exposure to communication skills had been entirely theoretical. Now, you should take the chance to fix that by doing practice for each of the communication skills we have covered.

For active listening, you and your spouse can listen to the radio or podcasts together. The catch is, one of you should quiz the other on little pieces of information they heard in the program to make sure they are really listening.

To practice controlling the emotional expression we make as part of nonverbal communication. We can look in a mirror with different facial expressions, imagining the emotions that go with them. Next, we can get these same emotions into our imaginations, but without showing them on our faces.

This powerful skill is called state control, and it is tremendously useful to prevent people from getting upset with the emotions they read on our faces.

State control is not taught nearly enough as a communication tool in therapy for couples, but it is an essential component of dialectical behavioral therapy. The reason for this is a simple misunderstanding. People think it is a means of washing all our emotions away and presenting a blank slate, but this isn't the case at all.

The more accurate way to understand state control is to look back on the days when you were a toddler. Back then, you didn't know any level of state control. No one did at that age. When you didn't get your way, you cried until you did. When you felt like crying or screaming, you just did it. You didn't let anyone stop you.

Everyone stops this childish lack of emotional control when they start adulthood at the least, which means everyone has some level of state control. The only difference is how much state control they have. There are a surprising number of people who can't seem to control any of the non-verbal signals that tell others what emotions they are feeling.

We may all have to learn a certain baseline of state control to be able to live in society, but that doesn't mean we're all equally good at it. Some people cannot seem to control themselves even into adulthood, and others seem as though they aren't affected by emotions at all.

All state control comes down to improving the control of the emotions you already have. Whether you have a lot or very little control of your emotions, you can make your emotions become less and less a part of your external presentation if you work at it.

Remember that state control doesn't mean not feeling how you feel. It means not showing it all to everyone. You already know how to do this somewhat from growing up; all you have to do is get even better at it.

All of the communication skills covered thus far can be practiced and reviewed. You and your spouse can practice them together to show each other you are serious about working through your fights.

Step 5 - INTIMACY AND SEX: OPENING UP WITHOUT SHAME AND KEEPING DESIRE ALIVE

Now it's time to take it to a new level and to improve aspects of your sex life as well. This is especially important for those who have been in a relationship with the same person for some time. Things may start to feel a bit dull and sex drives may not be as strong as they used to be. This is the perfect time to start rebuilding that sexual relationship with your partner by trying new things, communicating about personal desires, and playing fun games. We will be exploring the following topics; increasing couple intimacy, spicing up your sex life, trying new positions, playing new games and communicating your sexual wants/needs.

INCREASE COUPLE INTIMACY

As your relationship progresses, it is important to keep sex and lust alive, when you become progressively more and more comfortable with someone, it can take away some of the mystery, this is because there is no longer the excitement of getting to know a person and having everything you do together be brand new. At the beginning of a relationship, you are so eager to have sex with each other because the other person is new and hot and a novelty of sorts. As you get used to them, it can be easy to lose those feelings and settle into the comfortability of everything (like their body or your routine). This is by no means a bad thing. Getting to this point in your relationship is fun and comforting in its way, and is different from, but in some ways better than, the early stages. From a sexual perspective, though, we don't want the coming of this stage of your relationship to bring with it the end of exciting sex life.

If you are a long-term or married couple, you have likely tried every one of the classic sex positions together from missionary to 69. You have probably also developed a routine of your favorite positions and the order in which you do them by now. While you probably know how to please each other like it's second nature, rediscovering each other's bodies in a sexy way and learning new ways to pleasure each other is good for couples who have been together for a long time.

At the beginning of a relationship, you may have started having sex casually before you got together romantically, or you may have begun having sex when you became a couple. Either way, the beginning of any relationship comes with a lot of uncharted territories. You are exploring a new person's entire body- inside and out, and letting them see all of yours. Of course, this can be nerve-wracking. There will be some positions and sexual activities that you won't be completely comfortable doing with this person yet, even if you have done them before with someone else. There are certain positions you can stick to that are more comfortable at the beginning of a relationship, and that is best for getting to know someone's body and what they like. These positions serve us well when we are newly having sex with a person and are looking for the best way to help each other orgasm. You may think that you are well past this stage in a long-term relationship. This stage of discovery, however, is something that we want to return to every so often. This is because we want to rediscover the person's body and what they like as if it is the first time we are exploring it. People's desires change and their bodies change. It is important to continue to know how to pleasure your partner as they grow and change, and to expect the same from them for yourself. Further, revisiting our partner's body with an open mind as if we know nothing about it can be a fun and flirty way to renew zest in your sex life.

IMPORTANCE OF SPICING UP YOUR SEX LIFE

The main importance of spicing up your sex life is to increase intimacy between you and your partner. Not only does this help your sex life become more fun and exciting, but it also improves the communication and bond between you and your partner. We will be examining intimacy and the role that it plays in romantic relationships. We are going to look at how you can work to maintain intimacy with your partner and what achieving a greater level of intimacy can and will do for your relationship.

Intimacy is very important between two people when part of a couple, especially in the bedroom. Intimacy is what brings you close and keeps you close. Firstly, we will look at what intimacy means and the different types of intimacy that exist. There are different types of intimacy, and here I will outline them for you before digging deeper into the intimacy that exists between couples. Intimacy, in a general sense, is defined as mutual openness and vulnerability between two people. There are different ways in which you can give and receive openness and vulnerability in a relationship. Intimacy does not have to include a sexual relationship (though it can). Therefore, it is not only reserved for romantic relationships. Intimacy can also be present in other types of close relationships like friendships or family relationships. Below, I will outline the different forms of intimacy.

EMOTIONAL INTIMACY

Emotional intimacy is the ability to express oneself maturely and openly, leading to a deep emotional connection between people. Saying things like "I love you" or "you are very important to me" are examples of this. It is also the ability to respond in a mature and open way when someone expresses themselves to you by saying things like "I'm sorry" or "I love you too." This type of open and vulnerable dialogue leads to an emotional connection. For a deep emotional connection to form, there must be a mutual willingness to be vulnerable and open with one's deeper thoughts and feelings. This is where this type of emotional intimacy comes from.

INTELLECTUAL INTIMACY

Intellectual intimacy is a kind of intimacy that involves discussing and sharing thoughts and opinions on intellectual matters, from which they gain fulfillment and feelings of closeness with the other person. For example, if you are discussing politics with someone who you deem to be an intellectual equal, you may find that you feel a closeness with them as you share your thoughts and opinions and connect on an intellectual level. Many people find intellect and brains to be sexy in a partner!

SHARED INTERESTS AND ACTIVITIES

This form of intimacy is less well-known, but it is also considered a form of intimacy. When you share activities with another person that you both enjoy and are passionate about, this creates a sense of connection. For example, when you cook together or travel together. These shared experiences give you memories to share and this leads to bonding and intimacy (openness and vulnerability). This type of connection is usually present in friendships, in familial relationships, and more importantly, in romantic relationships. Being able to share interests and activities leads to a closeness that can be defined as intimacy.

PHYSICAL INTIMACY

Physical intimacy is the type that most people think of when they hear the term "intimacy," and it is the kind that we will be most concerned with within this workbook, as it is the type of intimacy that includes sex and all activities related to sex. It also involves other non-sexual types of physical contact such as hugging and kissing. Physical intimacy can be found in close friendships or familial relationships where hugging and kisses on the cheek are common, but it is most often found in romantic relationships.

Physical intimacy is the type of intimacy involved when people are trying to make each other orgasm. Physical intimacy is almost always required for orgasm. Physical intimacy doesn't necessarily mean that you are in love with the person you are having sex with; it just means that you are doing something intimate with another person physically.

It is also possible to be intimate with yourself, and while this begins with the emotional intimacy of self-awareness, it also involves the physical intimacy of masturbation and physical self-exploration. I define sexual, the physical intimacy of the self as being in touch with the parts of yourself physically that you would not normally be in touch with. If you are a woman, your breasts, your clitoris, your vagina, and your anus. If you are a man, your testicles, your penis, your anus. Being able to be physically intimate with yourself allows you to have more fulfilling sex, more fulfilling orgasms, and a more fulfilling overall relationship with your body. Allowing someone to be physically intimate with you in a sexual way is also an emotionally intimate experience, regardless of your relationship with the person. Being in charge of your own body while it is in the hands of another person is very important and this is why masturbation is such a key element to physical intimacy.

You can think of physical intimacy as something that breaks the barrier of personal space. By this definition, this includes touching of any sort, but especially sexual intercourse, kissing touching, and anything else of a sexual nature. When you are having sex with anyone, regardless of whether you have romantic feelings for them or not, you are having a physically intimate relationship with them. The difference between a relationship that involves physical intimacy alone and no other forms of intimacy and a romantic relationship is that a romantic relationship will also involve emotional intimacy, shared activities and intellectual intimacy is that a deep and lasting romantic relationship will need to include all of these forms of intimacy at once.

NEW POSITIONS TO TRY

When it comes to sex, changing the positions you use is the key to keeping it interesting and different. After a short time, a sexual routine can become boring and old, because you know what to expect at every turn and what to do next without thinking at all. Your brain, heart, and body do not need to be engaged like they are when you are doing something new and exciting that is turning you on. When you are performing a sex position that you have never tried before, your entire body is engaged, thinking about what is next, feeling new sensations, looking to the other person to see if they are feeling pleasure as well. This is very different from performing a position you have done many times over. This is why changing your sex positions is beneficial; it engages every part of you. I will be teaching you about a few new positions that you and your partner can try to spice things up a bit!

Step 6 - CHILDREN: HOW TO BECOME PARENTS TOGETHER

Parenting is a game-changer to all marriages. In many ways, it can change the relationship dynamic for the better or worse, depending on the specific set of circumstances. In television commercials featuring baby shower cards, diapers, and a litany of baby products, parenting, and marriage are depicted as pure bliss and effortless. Your relatives will sell you a story about how babies are a heaven-sent bundle of happiness – and they are – but they skip the hard work that goes into making it all work!

Of course, it is essential to love our children. But it is crucial to be alive to what parenting does to marriages. There is no reason that loving your child and working on your marriage should be mutually exclusive. A happy marriage almost always means a happy baby. Marriage happiness, sustainability, and worth are liked at the hip with parenting.

Studies into the relationship between marriage and parenting indicate that most relationships change for the worse when couples transition into families. Initially, caring for the baby means sleepless nights, a surge in demands in bringing up the baby, and an abundance of new expectations for both parents. The parents also have to hold down the requirements of a job. Between 30 and 50 percent of couples that become parents face massive stress and depression.

University of California, Berkeley researchers, establishes that more than 70 percent of all new mothers faced a marked decline in their marital satisfaction. Around one-third of new mothers and fathers experience substantial depression after becoming parenting. One-eighth of all couples that transition into parents experience divorce by the time their babies hit 18 months.

Shifting from lovers to parents can be tumultuous to your marriage. The transition shakes the foundations of your relations. The result is massive disruption of the normal flow of information between partners. It also upends the status quo of emotions and individual responsibilities. In short, there is a learning curve for the lovers when they become parents. Completing the learning and adjusting accordingly is vital to the success of parenting and marriage.

The emotional disruption is mainly driven by the changes in the typical social dynamics. For example, a working mom's life shifts from the bubbly office colleagues for breastfeeding, dealing with mountains of laundry, and bottle-washing. After around six months, she faces the prospect of changing back to her working routine. The husband has to work with the wife through the entire process. However, most fathers feel left out of the early years of caring for the child. The overall result is each of the spouses is doing more, the communication lines and frequency declines, and both feel massively underappreciated.

As the kid grows, you suddenly find yourself wondering about your child will be enrolled in the right preschool program. You worry whether your daughter or son is in the right music, art, and tumbling tots' classes.

Can Parenting be used to Strength Marriages?

It is not easy. It is difficult. But marriage can be used to sweeten your marriage, make it stronger, and long-lasting! Most people view parenting as a collection of stressors that will make your life miserable and probably accelerate the end of your relationship with your spouse. However, with the right touch, parenting can be the glue that holds you together. In this regard, it will benefit your relationship as well as the well-being of the kid(s).

All you can do to leverage parenting in improving your relationship within a marriage is to put your relationship first. Recognizing that your marriage is a work in progress goes a long way to cementing your commitment towards bolstering your bonds. Working on your differences consistently also helps strengthen the foundations of your relationship while ironing out disagreements before they become more significant issues.

A focus on appreciating each other while minimizing criticism is essential in sweetening your relationship. Communication is the underlying foundation of a relationship. Maintaining the bidirectional flow of information, opinions, views, and perspectives is necessary, retaining the enthusiasm to sustain a relationship of married spouses with a kid(s).

Using parenting as a tool to improve your relationship quality and sustainability needs a deliberate effort targeting the dynamics of parenting. Understanding the expected disruptions to the relationship parenting brings will help you be better prepared. It also means that you are better equipped to harness the parenting changes and making them work for your relationship.

Learning about parenting and preparing for the shifts it brings should include both spouses. This process must be collaborative firstly because both of you will need the knowledge and skills to maneuver through the impending changes. Secondly, a concerted approach is likely to succeed in maintaining a working and effective relationship. When both of you put in the work, you are susceptible to shoulder the burden equitably. Although parenting cannot biologically be equitable, it creates a sense that the husband is supportive of the wife during this period.

The challenge facing most couples going into marriage is that they are not prepared for the disruptions of parenting. They are not ready for the upending of their lives they face after the baby is born, and parenting begins. As a result, parenting becomes overwhelming, physically, and emotionally. This leads to a surge in conflicts and an increase in the likelihood of divorce or unhappy marriages/relationships.

Here are some suggestions on how you can use parenting as a platform to build a stronger and long-lasting relationship and marriage:

Talk about the Certainties and Uncertainties Ahead

Talking about uncertainties does not make them any more confident. However, it will help you be emotionally prepared and sure of yourself when navigating through the moments and circumstances of parenting.

It is also important to plan and ventilate some of the particular issues, such as splitting errands and household chores. It is essential to talk about where the income of the family will come from. In this case, it is crucial to answering the following questions: who is going to be the breadwinner? And who is going to stay at home rearing the child?

Talk about the day-care option. Establish who will get your baby to the day-care center and who will get him/her back. Explore the issue of a babysitter, the budget for this option, and plan your lives around what you agree. Figure out how night shift duties will be split, who is going to wash or sterilize the breast pump and bottles daily. Figure out the shopping schedule, cooking plan, and cleaning chores.

These details seem small and harmless. But without figuring out the division of labor regarding these aspects, they might contribute to frustration, stress, and depression. If left unsorted, they can gnaw away at the relationship.

However, figuring them out creates an understanding and collaborative approach that is healthy for your relationship. It also establishes a sense that everyone is doing their fair share. Moreover, developing a concise plan on dealing with these chores and duties reduces the chances that you will be overwhelmed as a couple when parenting begins. Emotionally, you will be prepared for the deluge of tasks and responsibilities, which will make it markedly more comfortable to handle and transition into the parenting role.

Focus on the Downside of Parenthood with the View of Avoiding its Pitfalls on the Marriage

Maintaining a positive and hopeful perception of parenting is important for new fathers and mothers. But it is vital to guard against lofty expectations that will be shattered by the reality of fatherhood and motherhood.

Yes, babies offer massive joy, and they bring a lot of happiness to a marriage. They also carry an uptick in physical and emotional exertions that can take their toll on the relationship. Bathing the baby, feeding, entertaining, and changing the baby 24 hours a day and 7 hours a week are demanding chores. All couples should be emotionally and physically prepared for such demands before they begin their roles as parents.

Focusing on and talking about the downside(s) of parenting is essential in marriage. It will help you to cope with the changes and disruptions to your lives. It is okay to talk about your fatigue, frustrations, and even anger with your spouse. Ensure, to be honest with your partner regarding these issues and also maintaining a supportive stance.

Feeling anger, frustration, and fatigue does not mean that you are a terrible parent. It is crucial to admit these emotions and focus on working together to resolve them within the marriage. This approach helps in disarming these emotions and thus prevents them from negatively affecting your relationship.

For example, you can agree in advance that if one of you is overwhelmed and is unable to fulfill their chores, the other will cover and take care of the baby for a while. This provides an option of relief for the overwhelmed partner. It also establishes a mutually supportive dynamic that deepens your affection for each other in the midst of a challenging period.

Fatigue, frustrations, and even anger resulting from anger can marinate into more significant issues within the marriage. For example, these emotions can easily lead to resentment of each other, lack of trust, and a communication breakdown. By focusing on constant and honest communication, you will always know how your partner is feeling at all times. You can render your support when they need it and shoulder some of their fear and uncertainty.

<u>Maintain Honesty about Gains and Losses</u>

In many instances, parenting will lead to some gains and losses. For example, you have gained the baby of your dreams. He/she melts your heart every time you see them. However, you cannot avoid feeling sad and empty because of the loss of your typical sex life. For the mother, you lost your sleek pre-baby size 8s and replaced them with elastic-waist jeans.

Most new parents typically complain, silently, about the disruption to their lives occasioned by the baby and their parenting duties and responsibilities. These complaints and silent resentment cause the marital distance to widen. In some extreme instances, it can lead to shame and a decline in self-esteem.

For example, a new daddy might feel replaced by the baby in his spouse's life and affection. The mother might be frustrated and even sad about the ways parenting (pregnancy, nursing, and the rigors of childcare) have transformed her body. These feelings are normal among new parents.

Sharing such feelings of loss, shame, or disruption is vital in dealing with the emotional toll of parenting. Maintaining honesty about these issues with your partner helps you to feel better and strengthen your bond as a couple.

Communication regarding these feelings helps establish a perspective for behavior. For example, feelings of loss might make the mother snappy and frustrated, which might spill over to her interactions with other people, including the husband. The husband might also display emotions and reactions that are out of the norm.

Through communication and honesty, you will sort through these emotions and explain the context of behavior. The resulting understanding will create rigor room for a learning curve and some space for the growth and development of your relationship.

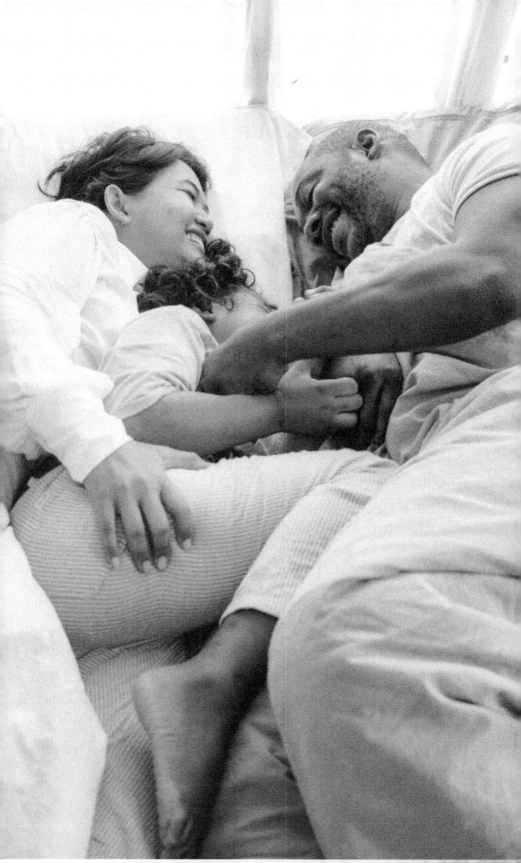

Step 7 - WORK AND FINANCES: RESPECT EACH OTHER'S WORK NEEDS AND FIND A FAIR COMPROMISE, DECIDING TOGETHER HOW TO INVEST YOUR MONEY

When a man and a woman are living as a couple, or when they have a wedding project, it is rare to hear them discuss the topic of financial management. However, according to several studies, the monetary question is at the origin of several divorces. Being in a relationship is not just about love. It's nice to love each other, but it does not pay for shopping, cinema, or traveling in Beijing. So how do you manage your money in a relationship? Of course, as there is no one way to be in love, there is no miracle recipe for managing one's finances with one's life partner. That may be why we sometimes see marvelous relationships that end in violent conflict because of money. Thus, to avoid those money management problems which are a real wasp nest for your marriage, here are some tips.

<u>Set priorities</u>

In the life of a couple, it is perfectly reasonable and understandable that everyone can have different habits and desires than the other. And it is normal to try to answer them reasonably, without penalizing one or the other. Only, it must be noted that life as a couple requires a certain number of choices, even sacrifices. It's therefore imperative to know how to make choices while taking into consideration the desire of each other.

50

Also, it is vital, and above all, to define the way of working together, to establish a budget, even prematurely, and to think about savings and investments. It is normal for couples to divide their daily tasks to make their lives easier. However, when it comes to your financial strategy, it's important to talk about it and choose a line to follow. You probably have joint projects that require individual and collective sacrifices on which you will have to agree. Listening is the best way to getting along.

The three healthy ways of spending in a relationship: The financial management of the couple is a spectrum that is built around three methods: equity, half and a half, and pooling. There is a brilliant idea when both of you agree. Fairness means that everyone participates according to their income. Sometimes one spouse earns significantly more than the other or has special needs; it can, therefore, contribute more than the latter without this being unfair. Half and a half is the method that will prevail when both members of the couple have the same financial personality (debt, leisure, income). They will share the expenses. Pooling is acting without regard to who pays what. The couple serves as a single entity in revenues and expenditures.

Communicating with your spouse

Even if one decides to have separate accounts and finances, it is essential to talk with one's spouse about everything related to investments (loans and outstanding debts). And this is all the more important since a standard account has been created. You should not have financial secrets. Having secret accounts could be the source of unpleasant surprises.

Moreover, if one of the two partners disappeared or is deceased. An obnoxious assumption but still possible, being aware of the reports and accounts of the deceased simplifies the life of the survivor.

Create a common account

To put into practice the three healthy ways of financial management, couples will have to choose how they will manage their money in a financial institution. This comes down to three choices too: joint account, a separate account, or both.

Separate accounts allow seeing the expenses and contribution of each. Each spouse can, therefore, bear his share of responsibility and the balance is quickly found. However, this solution may sometimes not be optimal. A couple is also a two-person adventure that involves a lot of shared expenses. Tracking can become complicated. The joint account makes it easier to keep track of the couple's expenses. For those who wish to pool their money, this can be a good solution. That said, the joint account requires more control and consultation to avoid unpleasant surprises. But, while maintaining a certain autonomy and a personal financial space, it is possible to spend together for joint projects. This is the best of both systems but also concentrates on their faults. It will require more logistics.

The creation of a standard account makes it possible to simplify the participation of each one in the ordinary expenses and the follow-up of the costs and the budget. Then you have to feed the account for the ordinary expenses. Each spouse has, of course, the freedom to keep a personal account, which he can manage independently by keeping a discretionary income.

As for the management of this account, we must try to allocate the funds to the common priorities. We must also try to be rigorous, but without depriving ourselves of everything. This would mean that if one spouse needs something that does not jeopardize the couple's finances, the other spouse should allow him or her to buy it.

Once you have made the financial decisions, you can go about your relationship without worrying more than you need to about money. In the end, good accounts make good relationships.

<u>Balancing the budget</u>

Achieve and maintain a balanced budget by dividing ordinary expenses based on each person's income. As an illustration, if one of the two spouses earns 10,000 dollars while the other earns 5,000 dollars, the one who makes more should assume two-thirds of the domestic expenses, while the other one would pay just the remaining third.

As soon as the situation of the couple evolves, it is necessary to adjust and adapt to the budget. This is, for example, the case when the family is growing or when buying a house. Moreover, not living beyond one's means is an excellent way to reach a balanced budget, evoked just above, to build precautionary savings, and to reserve an investment capacity.

But we must at all costs limit purchases on credit and, above all, question its consumption habits. Small daily and recurring expenses can be nice sums for which you could find a better use.

If one of the spouses is thrifty while the other is a spender, try to find the balance by defining the tasks of each. In other words, it is imperative to establish who does what. The ideal would be a good manager who deals with the management of high finances. But communication must remain, that the decision-making remains shared and that the other can assume other responsibilities in the couple.

Also, even if you do not have investment projects, a financial advisor can be of great help to you. You can start with your banker, for example. To be satisfied with your only banker is however not judicious. The best thing in finance is still to be trained. You could be autonomous and keep control of your investments.

Contrary to what you can imagine, it is not so complicated. And many sites and blogs are very well done and provide good advice. If not wholly independent, training will also help you better understand the advice and suggestions of your financial advisor, ask relevant questions, and be surer of your choices.

Money can be a source of trouble and discord in your marriage. Take the lead, and these tips should help you.

One last tip: do not hesitate to address the subject, even if you fear being taken for someone interested. In any case, the question of money will come sooner or later. So go!

Moreover, by explaining your approach, doubts will be lifted. And then you will pass for someone responsible and proactive.

Step 8 - HOW TO FACE AND SOLVE CONFLICTS

I will be teaching you the importance of conflict resolution and how to do it peacefully. As we all know, every relationship will come across conflict and its own set of arguments. How you approach to conflict is extremely important as it can make or break your relationship. We will be focusing on all topics related to conflict resolution; the importance of them, coping with solvable relationship problems, violent communication, and nonviolent communication, learning to use nonviolent communication during conflicts, and restoring trust after conflict. Remember, conflicts are normal within relationships and the purpose isn't to avoid any conflict possible. The point is to accept that conflicts do happen but to learn how to navigate through them so that you and your partner can find a solution to strengthen the relationship.

CONFLICT RESOLUTION SKILLS ARE IMPORTANT

Since conflict and arguments are an unavoidable part of life, it is important to learn how to communicate yourself during situations like that. While it may seem like there are a lot of things to remember, it will come more naturally the more you practice it. This will focus on providing you with techniques and examples on how to express yourself during arguments and conflicts. Making judgments, blaming, yelling, shaming, and so on are types of communication styles that you don't want to use during conflicts. As long as you remember these points, you will be able to express yourself in a nonviolent way and the steps will come back to your memory. Even if you are not following the steps too closely, as long as you are ensuring that you are not using violent communication, you will be much closer to using nonviolent communication than if you had forgotten everything you learned entirely.

VIOLENT COMMUNICATION VS. NONVIOLENT COMMUNICATION

We will look at the difference between violent and nonviolent communication so that you have an idea of how to tell them apart. Now that you know what communication is on a basic level, we can dive a little bit deeper and learn the difference between these two methods of communication. There is a very thin line between violent and non-violent communication, in order for a person to learn how to communicate non-violently, they must be able to distinguish the two. Let's dive right in.

Oftentimes while communicating, especially in times of conflict, people will use means of communication that can be considered "violent." While this does not mean physical violence, we can be violent in the way that we communicate. What this means is communicating in a way that results in harm to someone else or ourselves. Violent communication is a means of communication that includes any number of the following;

- Judging

- Shaming

- Criticizing

- Ridiculing

- Demanding

- Coercing

- Labeling

- Threatening

- Blaming

- Accusing

When any or all of the following are present in our communications, we are using violent communication. Communicating in this way has negative impacts on the people with whom we are communicating. As this is violent communication, it causes internal harm. If we are communicating intrapersonally in this way, we may cause harm to ourselves. If we communicate in this way with others, we can cause internal harm to others. In time, this type of communication can lead to anger and resentment, and if we speak to ourselves in this way, it can eventually lead to depression.

Oftentimes, we don't even know we are using violent communication, as it may be quite a normal way of interacting for us. Many societies model violent communication and thus, the people who grow up in them don't realize that there is any other way to communicate. This causes many interactions to be full of anger and hate and involve raised voices and harsh words. Sometimes, this leads to physical violence.

Violent communication aims to lower a person's feelings of self-worth, ignores their needs, and is void of compassion. It can happen on both the part of the speaker and the listener. Below are some examples of different forms of violent communication for your reference.

1. Moral Judgement or Evaluation

"Jennifer is lazy."

In this example, the speaker is using judgment. They are also labeling Jennifer and being critical of her. They are evaluating her and doing so in a judgmental way. In this type of violent communication, the speaker often sees the other person as being wrong.

2. Denying Responsibility

"It's not my fault; the policy states that I have to fire you."

In this example of violent communication, the speaker is refusing to take responsibility for their actions and blaming them on policies, regulations, and rules. In this type of example, the person may also blame their thoughts or feelings on other people or rules, social rules, or anything other than their decision-making.

3. Demanding

"You need to do my homework for me."

In this type of example, the speaker is implying (or sometimes explicitly stating) that there is the threat of punishment, of having to take the blame, or of losing a reward if they do not comply with the demand. This type can also be seen in the reverse, where there is the implication of a reward if the person complies with the demand. This is a manipulative form of communication which is also a type of demand.

4. Lack of Compassion

THE DIFFERENCE BETWEEN VIOLENT AND NONVIOLENT COMMUNICATION

As you now have seen each type of communication on their own, we are going to compare them. Violent communication tends to be the type that we turn to automatically and is the one that is modeled for us when we enter the world as children. On the television, on public transit, and even in our homes growing up, we are exposed to violent communication. A person is rarely able to conduct themselves using only nonviolent communication in a world that answers them with violent communication, but it is possible.

Violent communication approaches interactions using negative assumptions and judgments toward other people, and everything that is said comes from these assumptions.

When one person approaches an interaction in this way, the other person or people tend to get defensive and they will then also use violent communication. The result is hurt feelings, feelings of inadequacy, feeling judged and shamed, among others. These people who left this interaction feeling these ways then approach their next interaction using violent communication because they are still feeling hurt by their last interaction. The cycle then continues as the hurt feelings and anger are passed from one person to the next over and over again.

On the contrary, when a person approaches an interaction from a place of emotional vulnerability and being open to discovering the other people in the interaction instead of judging them, the other people will tend to respond by also showing emotional vulnerability and genuine concern for the well-being of others. When this is passed on from interaction to interaction instead of violent communication and anger, people leave with positive feelings instead of negative ones.

Changing the interactions that you have with people is not easy, especially if you feel judged or shamed by the words of others. It takes one person in the interaction to be brave enough to approach it in a loving and genuine way to turn it around, and this is how NVC can spread.

In a long-term relationship such as that between spouses or partners, the type of communication you use can have a great impact on the health and longevity of your relationship. Not only in times of conflict but in everyday interactions with your partner, the way that you approach their feelings and their needs creates quite an impact in the long term. It has been shown that the longevity of a marriage is largely dependent on the ability of the partners to recognize the needs of the other and help them in meeting those needs. This ties into nonviolent communication as it focuses heavily on the needs of people and the feelings that are associated with them. By using compassion and a genuine interest in helping your partner improve their well-being, you will have a healthy and thriving relationship.

The other part of this is how your relationship affects your children. The first relationship that is modeled for a child is the relationship between their parents. By using nonviolent communication with each other, you are modeling a healthy and respectful, deep and loving relationship. This idea of how a relationship looks is something that your child will take with them for the rest of their life and will form their expectations and ideas of how they will conduct themselves in their relationship one day. It is important to be mindful of this if you have children.

LEARNING NONVIOLENT COMMUNICATION DURING CONFLICTS

Nonviolent communication can be used to resolve many types of conflicts. These problems can be things like deciding who takes your dog for a walk or telling your child to do their homework. While these do not need to be conflicts, sometimes, through the use of violent communication, they can turn into them. By using nonviolent communication, you can stop this before it happens. For example:

If you and your partner are deciding who is going to take your dog for a walk:

"The dog needs to go out for a walk before bed. Having to walk him before bed makes me feel anxious because I have to wake up early in the morning and I need sleep. Would you be willing to take him for his before-bed walk?"

Or:

If you are telling your child to do their homework:

"Your homework has to be done before tomorrow. Seeing you playing video games makes me worried because I value education. Would you be willing to do your homework after dinner before playing more video games?"

Either of these situations has the potential to turn into a much bigger conflict, but by approaching it using nonviolent communication, you can prevent this and even diffuse the situation before it becomes any sort of conflict. Using nonviolent communication for problem-solving can be seen as a way to discuss matters calmly and can help to make any sort of decision or discuss anything.

When confronted with a conflict, you would want to practice non-violent communication. What nonviolent communication does differently than other methods of conflict resolution or problem solving is that it aims to resolve a situation to the satisfaction of all parties without having to compromise. It aims to promote understanding and compassion instead of the hurt and judgment that is usually a result of the confrontation. Nonviolent communication diffuses situations even before they become heated and prevents conflicts altogether. By having everyone express themselves through nonviolent communication, situations are resolved well before anger has built up to the point of an outburst.

Conflict is not an inherently negative or violent thing. It does not have to lead to the breakdown of relationships of any kind or yelling and screaming. It does not have to involve a dominant party and a submissive party or an expresser and a listener. Conflict can be seen positively in that it can promote voicing one's thoughts and speaking the truth. This is how situations and relationships can be improved rather than harmed.

Step 9 - EVERYDAY LIFE AND THE POWER OF SMALL GESTURES

When relationships age, couples often feel like caring has gone out of the relationship. By showing how much, you care, you are letting your spouse know that you value your relationship and hope to make the most of it. It may not be easy to find the little ways to show them that you do care, but the little things can go a long way when used correctly.

What are some ways that you can show your spouse that you care for them? Think of any way you can, big or small. It's often the little things that make your life much more meaningful. I'm going to give you some suggestions on some ways to show your spouse that you do care!

Making His or Her Favorite Meal

You can show your spouse that you care about them by knowing what foods they like and when they want them. Make an effort to prepare these foods and make it a romantic date. By doing small things like this, you show your spouse that you do care and that you have taken the effort to prove it. Not only are you doing something to show caring, but you have also demonstrated that you know your spouse in a more profound way.

Leaving Love Letters

A simple love letter left in a random place can make someone's day. Try using a scrap of paper and writing something sweet on it and placing it in a place where you know that your spouse will find it. This can make them smile and let them know that you do care about them enough to think about them in small ways.

Saying "I love you."

Even though love is typically shown, saying that you love your spouse will not go unnoticed. By telling them that they are loved shows them that you are thinking about them at the moment and care enough to let them know that. So, the next time that you are in the same room as your spouse give them a little love and tell them how much you do love them.

Making an Extra Effort to Accommodate Needs

One of the hugest complaints of marriage is that the other partner never meets the other's needs. Needs can be extensive and varying, but taking the time to know what your spouse needs and how you can accommodate them will help you to show that you do pay attention and are willing to go the extra steps to make sure that your spouse is happy and well-taken care. Don't discount small needs because they can make A significant difference in the way you and your spouse treat one another!

Doing Little Things That the Other Enjoys

You may hate that your spouse loves to watch Monday night football or other small things. However, taking the time to do these activities with your spouse will show them that you really do take an interest in them and that you care enough to spend the time with them, even if it is an activity that you don't enjoy. Sucking it up and doing something you may not necessarily enjoy for an hour or two won't kill you, and the benefits to your marriage can show due to your time spent.

Showing your partner that you do notice them and care for the little parts of who they are can help you to grow closer. As time goes by, and we become comfortable in our marriages, we find that we tend to let the little things slip through the cracks. It takes a small amount of time to show your spouse that you do care and that you are willing to go the extra mile to do something that they enjoy.

Being Romantic

Believe it or not, romance isn't dead. Even though it may seem like it's a think of the past for you, you will find that there are ways to rekindle the spark that romance played in your life when you first met your spouse. It can be challenging to find ways to be romantic when you know your spouse well, but adding an element of surprise to what you do can go a long way in showing your spouse that you still have it in you.

What things do you consider romantic? Try using those ideas when it comes to romancing your spouse. Depending on the other's gender, some of the ideas will work better than others. Let's take a look at some ways that you can be romantic without having to put tons of effort into it.

Candle Lit Dinner

It might seem a little cliché, but a candlelit dinner is incredibly romantic and allows you and your spouse some downtime after a long and stressful day. You don't have to cook a gourmet meal to make this a possibility. Set a table for two with candles and eat your dinner to some soft and romantic music while you let the pressures from your day slip away.

Flowers and Candy

Guys and girls alike really like a pleasant surprise of flowers and candy. However, you have to know your partner well to know whether or not this is something that they would genuinely enjoy. Some guys might think it silly and sappy. You may enjoy it, so let your spouse know that this is something that they can do for you. Romance goes both ways, so having a one-sided effort on bringing passion into your marriage will not work. Encourage your spouse to try some of these ideas as well.

Favorite Restaurant

Everyone has a favorite restaurant unless you are married to a person who hates to go out. Know what your spouse's favorite restaurant is and go and surprise him or her with a treat. This simple gesture will show that you do know them well and that you are willing to go the extra steps to make sure that they are happy and cared for. Depending on the restaurant, this can be a romantic date night. Do whatever you can to make the outing special.

Cards for No Reason

Greeting cards are an excellent way to show that you care and love someone. A card for no reason can brighten a day and make someone feel special. The significant part is that you can get cards in a variety of ways. There are ecards, paper cards, or you can even make your cards. Also, they come with different messages for different reasons. Find something that will suit the situation and use it to show your significant other that you are thinking about him or her!

Random Shows of Affection

Sometimes the one spark that you need in your relationship is affection. Your spouse may feel as though you don't care because you never show him or her love any longer. Don't allow this problem to affect your relationship. A simple kiss on the cheek or a hug can show your spouse that you still care and that they always mean something to you.

Being romantic can be the gateway to passion. You may have to teach yourself how to show affection and caring by being romantic before you can hope to have that passion in your marriage reignite. Try different methods to be romantic with your spouse. The efforts won't go unnoticed, and your spouse will know that you are thinking about them and your relationship. Don't be afraid of romance. You married your spouse for a reason, and romance will help you to maintain a healthy and robust relationship.

Bringing Passion Back

Once you have mastered being romantic, passion can be quick to follow. Passion stems from romance. It's a sign of wholehearted and devoted love that lets the world know that you genuinely love and care for the person that you're married to. True passion is a dedicated love that shows in your actions and your words towards your spouse. Do you still love your spouse, wholeheartedly? Are you ready to show the world how you feel?

True passion can be a difficult concept for some people to grasp and apply to their relationships. If you're one of these people, then a few suggestions may help you in showing the world how much you care for your partner. Not only will you show passion to others, but you can also show passion in private!

Holding Hands and Showing Affection

You may mock the young kids who have to be holding their companion's hand continually. They seem silly and foolish, but hand-holding does much more than show affection. It shows that the person by your side belongs to you and that you won't let him or her go. By being somewhat possessive, you are showing your partner that you are still in love with him or her and willing to fight for your relationship.

Bringing the Sparks Back into Your Love Life

The sparks in your relationship might feel as though they had faded years ago. Your spouse may have become the one that provides companionship for you, and they don't do a whole lot else. However, bringing back ways that can spark romance will help bring those sparks back into your relationship. Try the small things and ease your way into the passionate life once more. It may never be the way it was when you first met and fell in love, but this new romance can be bigger and better if you allow it to be!

Openly Displaying Your Needs and Emotions

Sometimes your spouse has no idea that you need caring and emotion. You know each other so well that you can easily sidestep these thoughts and feelings without it being a big deal. Needs and emotions are a big deal. Try showing your spouse that you need and want these from him or her. You don't have to come across as incredibly needy, show them that you would like a little love and companionship.

Valuing Each Other's Company

You never know when your spouse will not be there. Several things can happen in life to make it so that you are no longer together. Frequently, people divorce because they feel as though their spouses don't care for them any longer. If more people were to value their spouses and the company they provide more often, many marriages could be saved, and love could live. Take the time to spend time with your spouse. Show your spouse that you want to be there and that you value your time together. This can make a massive difference in the passion in your relationship.

Passion is something that seems to happen naturally when a relationship is new and fades over time. However, passion is what probably brought you into your relationship, so it will be something that you don't want to lose. Take the time to grow and nourish the passion in your marriage and your relationships.

It doesn't matter how long you have been married or how old you are. There will always be an opportunity to show your spouse that you still love and are passionate about your relationship. Just because it feels as though that point in your relationship has ended, don't allow it to fade. There are always new and creative ways to rekindle the passion and romance that your first relationship had. Don't be afraid of the romance changes over time. Just find ways in which you can show your love and your devotion to your spouse daily.

Once you have discovered the passion in your marriage once more, you will be prepared to enjoy each other and your life together again. You may have had parts that you still enjoyed. Keep those in your grasp and build new parts around them. Passion isn't about the hot and heavy feelings that you feel when your first meet a person. It's about showing love and devotion to them regularly.

Step 10 - SPIRITUAL LIFE AND GRATITUDE

A prayer could be referred to as a sacred relationship shared with the omnipotent God Almighty. It could as well be referred to as an unseen contact developed by meditating and permanent self-surrender. In prayer, we lay our pains, tears, and needs before God Almighty. We believe/trust in Him. Prayers help and give us comfort.

Through prayer, we can express our gratitude for the blessings we have been able to achieve over a specific period. Prayer could also be said to be a time when we can put our most confidential toil, anguish, and anxieties in God's presence and then feel better.

Virtually, the more we pray, the more we learn how to earnestly forge our partner, respect, trust, love, and share moments of pain as well as happiness sincerely with each other in a relationship. A family that considers praying together prospers together in that light.

<u>Kinds of prayer</u>

There are different kinds of prayer, but in this context, only those that are related to relationships are the ones that would be emphasized for the sake of understanding.

Family prayer - Family prayer is a sort of prayer that is regularly done in a family. In this sort of prayer, the family members are the main participants. Guests, neighbors, or employees of the household could become a part of it. Family prayer is widely led by the most senior in the household, the father in the family. It is ideally considered and practiced twice daily, preferably, or usually in the morning and the evening. It could include a reading from the scripture or Bible or any other Holy workbook and then explained or discussed. It could include the regular prayers coupled with thanksgiving or praising songs, from the hymn workbook. A prayer offering for the welfare and togetherness of each of the family members often brings love in the hearts of either partner toward each other. Thanksgiving or any special prayer could as well be allowed in family prayers. Prayer time is often regarded or seen as a sacred time, and all family members should be able to recognize it based on routine. A family prayer would help all members in staying together in hard or difficult times of life. It makes tolerating and forgiving each other a lot easier. It teaches love as well as helps to stay in harmony with each other. It has the power to rejuvenate a shattered relationship slowly.

Personal/individual prayer – this kind of prayer could be termed or defined as personal/individual contact or communication with God. In other words, it is referred to as well as the most sacred time shared with God whenever it is done. It is a kind of prayer that allows one to be able to get rid of all the worries and then get relaxed for a while. It is a single time or moment of solitude and meditation when one acknowledges God's touch and His power closely. This wonderful time spent with God helps and strengthens one's potential and fills him/her with the confidence to encounter the real struggles of life with enthusiasm. A plea to God for companionship can be a prayer intended for the family members, strength, or might to forgive dear ones or it can be a request in reuniting a broken relationship. It ends with thanksgiving for a wonderful life, an awesome family or household, and for all the blessings that are being received.

A fasting prayer is often done in times of sickness, pain, utter confusion, and need of direction and to overcome the struggles of life such as relationship matters. It is often commonly done during the "Lenten" period for the Christians, a period of fasting and self-restraint. It is essential to do fasting prayers in the time of lent. It aids in building a strong connection with God. Lent is a sacred time in the time every Christian should give quality time to the Lord God every day. It is a good idea to switch to a vegetarian diet during this holy period. Fasting prayers have to be done in utter sincerity repentance can have a supernatural effect. It could help the heart-broken people to find peace as well as solace. The sort of prayers helps and spreads peace and coordination among the family members, most directly, husband and wife. It often helps to enhance the spiritual state of each member.

Genuine prayer offerings from the core of the heart, for grace, health, direction, and strength, are very efficient and are always answered by God, helping in His infinite mercy. Miracles, maturity, and understanding play a vital role in stopping valuable relationships from getting ruined or shattered. Despair vanishes. Prayers help and bind families in love and yield spiritually alert and loving members.

The life of the family is precious and should not be permitted to shatter. This aspect was deliberate in explaining what a prayer is and how it could aid family members to stay united in love, peace, and harmony. You would realize how prayers could restore broken relationships and then prevent the destruction of a family that was meant to thrive until 'eternity.'

Step 11 - BECOME AN EXPERT ABOUT YOUR PARTNER

When you are just getting married, you have nothing but each other. This is the point where you focus on the most important building blocks of marriage so that your relationship is not solid, but also healthy and long-lasting. However, as your relationship continues to grow and expand, lots of stuff accumulates and becomes a distraction from what is truly essential.

Soon, you stop looking at the value of the relationship, and you focus more on the value of the home. We start saving for retirement and children's college funds that we forget to pay attention to the health of our marriage. We spend lots of time in the garage taking care of the car that we forget to spend time in bed with the one we love.

This is what I refer to as clutter. They first steal your family's attention, then money and time. What is left is very little that the marriage cannot stand strong and begins to crumble down one building block at a time.

You must wise up and start realizing that material things will not help your marriage stay strong and long-lasting. Your home, car, and retirement account can be very nice, but you don't need them to make your marriage a success. Here are essential building blocks you need to cultivate in your marriage;

Love and Commitment

This is the core of your marriage. When you choose to love your partner and marry them, what you are saying is that you are committing to taking them into your life. Love and commitment are traits that go far beyond fleeting emotions portrayed in the movies, romance novels, and big screen TV series.

Realize that feelings will come and go, but what will stay forever is your decision to commit to each other until the end of time. This is precisely what defines a healthy, strong, and long-lasting marriage.

Sexual faithfulness

This is something that most people do not quite understand its true meaning. When you talk about sexual faithfulness, it goes beyond our bodies as couples. It involves what we see with our eyes, mind, soul, and heart. When you get married to your spouse, everything you have is theirs and should not be shared with anyone else.

This means that you cannot have sexual fantasies about someone other than your spouse. Marriage means sacrificing all your sexual faithfulness and fantasies to your partner alone. When you choose to offer moments of sexual intimacy to anyone other than your spouse, you are sacrificing your sexual faithfulness to them.

To build a strong marriage, you must guard your sexuality daily. You have to devote it to your spouse alone. To be sexually faithful to your spouse, you must cultivate a sense of self-discipline and awareness of what consequences you will face if you did the contrary. Choose to resist putting anything before your eyes, body, and heart that will compromise your faithfulness to your spouse.

Humility

The truth is that no one is perfect in this world. We all have flaws and weaknesses. What is even more interesting is that relationships reveal these flaws and weaknesses faster than any other institution on earth. One of the most important building blocks of a strong and healthy marriage is the ability to admit that you are far from being perfect. Accept that you make mistakes and that you need forgiveness.

When you choose to hold an attitude of being superior to your spouse, you are inviting resentment into your relationship. This is exactly what will stand in the way of a long-lasting marriage.

Do you sometimes look down upon your partner? Do you think that you are more important than they are? If you are a victim of this, you need to take a step back and find where you went wrong. Go back to the crossroads and find your way back. Take a pen and write down all the things you love about your spouse. This exercise will help you stay humble. Do this as often as you can, and you will keep your marriage in check!

Patience and Forgiveness

Getting into marriage with your partner means that two very different people are choosing to come together to be joined as one thing! Does it mean that you both have similar beliefs and values? Does it mean that you both will like how your partner does things?

Not!

It is about accommodating your spouse and learning ways to show them unending forgives and patience. It is about choosing to admit with humility when you are wrong and stop expecting that your partner is perfect. It is choosing to let go of past mistakes and faults rather than holding your partner hostage.

You cannot build a long-lasting relationship if every time there is a mistake that is made, you see revenge. If you keep holding on to past hurt, you are never going to focus your effort on what is best for your relationship. Today, choose to let go of your partner's past mistakes and forgive them. Forgiveness is the best way you are going to set your heart free and your relationship free, healthy, and happy.

Time

There is no way you are going to do your marriage work if you don't invest time in it. You have to realize that this is something that has never happened and will never see the light of day.

A successful relationship requires that you become intentional in your actions and invest quality time with your partner. The truth is, when you have no quantity of time, it can be hard to have quality time.

Realize that the relationship you have with your partner requires intimacy. It is a deep relationship that requires you to have your whole being invested in it, and that includes your time.

While there are so many responsibilities we have outside our marriage, it is important to note when all else is lost, the one place you go back is home. This means that you have to look for ways you can make spending time with your spouse. Do date nights, picnics, and coffee dates with them every often. This is how you stay in each other's lives.

Honesty and trust

One thing that you need to realize is that building trust in a relationship takes time. You can choose to be selfless, patient, committed, and faithful, but trust is something that you have to nurture over time. It can take weeks, months, or years to have it. It starts with you being yourself and doing the things you said you would do.

Because it takes time, you better get started now!

If you need to rebuild your trust in a relationship, you must start working even harder than you have before.

Communication

When you are in a healthy marriage, it means that you communicate effectively and openly with your spouse as much as possible. However, you don't stop at that; you go as far as communicating with each other what your dreams, fears, desires, and hopes are. You not only share the changes that your kids are going through but also changes taking place in your hearts and souls.

Realize that having honest and forthright communication with your spouse is the key foundation to a strong, healthy, and long-lasting marriage. Being married means, you are both joined together into one thing. Therefore, stop keeping secrets from your other self. Start communicating openly and without judgment with your spouse and watch how your bond grows stronger than you have ever imagined.

Selflessness

Even though this is a trait that will never show up on any marriage survey, the truth is that most marriages are broken because of selfishness. Most studies will hide it in finances, infidelity, lack of commitment, and even incompatibility, but the bottom line is selfishness. The reason why you choose to cheat on your spouse is that you only care about your feelings and not what your partner will feel.

The truth is that when you are selfish, you only care about yourself and you alone. That is why instead of choosing to forgive your spouse, you resent them and lack patience with them.

Today, I will challenge you to give your hopes, dreams, anxieties, fears, and life to your partner. Start living life together. This is a very simple call for you to start valuing your marriage and your partner. Instead of resenting them, choose to accept them, and be patient with them. Care for them and invest you're all in them daily.

Trust me; when you do what I am asking you to do, you will see the worth in it at the end of the day. Remember that a successful, healthy, and strong relationship is more important than all the temporal material things people tend to focus on. And this is something that will last longer even when all else is gone!

Step 12 - COMMON RELATIONSHIP MISTAKES AND MAKING MARRIAGE A SUCCESS

Every marital relationship begins with lots of hope as well as dreams about a life-long connection filled with ardor and togetherness.

Only a few marriages do fulfill the hopes of the participants and bring together a complete state of mind.

Why?

We are too wrapped up or even buried in the ideology of the body as who we are because, as humans, we cannot be perfect.

There are a lot of serious reasons for this, but here a few are being singled out.

- Getting married just for the sake of affection or love without first inspecting or considering the depth of love

Devoting to a long-term relationship like marital relationships solely only based on that feeling of love is an error.

Romantic mood 'dies' as time advances and far more important concerns such as 'values,' 'household background', 'creed/faith', 'financial capability' come about.

These problems are of genuine significance that practically several individuals with feelings of wholly-shared affection ignore.

- Getting married to someone who does not share a hobby or an interest.

While marital relationships with a person who does not share an interest or hobby do not itself allow the marriage to be unstable, the presence of such an interest in what the other person considers with passion or pastime could make life more delightful for both the partners for a very long time if not forever.

And this could make a genuine distinction so while picking a life partner, this element or factor should be considered very well.

For some reason or other, this element is often ignored before marriage. And efforts begin right after marriage to regulate the partner to one's concern or establish a different common interest.

While that is not a difficult job, the process of correcting may become un-palatable and might lead to an unstable marriage experience.

When bearing in mind is compatibility, not directly knowing what questions to think over.

Believing mindful and suitable queries may offend him or her. One might think that excessive exploration of a future partner's history or background might not be a good idea.

As the other partner in the relationship might discover, this sort of believed technique keeps numerous couples from asking the ideal notions before considering a marital or relationship a lifelong business.

- Relying way too much on a friend or loved ones' approval

A good number of couples in a relationship often get married based on the recommendation of friends.

While relatives and good friends are typically considered as well-wishers, taking their suggestion or position is not always the best idea.

As their acknowledgment of an individual could never equal the understanding, the person has about herself or himself.

The person to be married is in a much better state to pick a compatible life partner for himself or herself.

- Getting hooked/married all in the name of pleasing others such as parents, friends, etc.

Often, people get married just to make someone else happy. It might be the shotgun type with the parent(s) insisting. There is no big issue in making somebody pleased, yet only if that would not jeopardize one's marital relationship, such as happiness and self-will.

As an effect, one may wind up marrying someone who is not suitable and if this is the situation, how to save a relationship tomorrow would likely not be repairable.

Enriching and loving experiences with each other helps us side with completeness more so than separation. Moreover, you will need to be mindful of the above factors so that your marriage will last a lifetime.

OVERWHELMING SAD FEELING AND LONELINESS IN A RELATIONSHIP

Some people today are in a 'partnership', but the same is lonely. Most of the time, it is because they went into the relationship for the sake of putting an end to loneliness. Entering a relationship with someone just for the company is not extremely wise.

Getting into a relationship with somebody just for not being by yourself could trigger issues down the line.

Let us say that you decide to get involved with someone based on those impressions, and you get married. There is a higher tendency that your home would not be enjoyable as there would be a tendency of feeling sad and lonely in such a relationship. Imagine being alone again as you are with someone that you could barely tolerate due to crazy differences between both of you. This is possible as the person might not have the requirements to match your expectations.

Make smart choices before getting to the point where you are in a relationship but find yourself lonely. Do not allow solitude to become an issue in your relationships.

Nonetheless, if we must assume that you have found yourself in this situation, how do you survive? One of the best things to do in the position of loneliness or feeling sad and lonely in a relationship could be answered by making efforts to spend some time with animals such as a dog or cat. That might help you in overcoming the issues of loneliness and depression.

You could also get a hobby or begin to make a search on your heart for that thing you naturally love doing.

If you are feeling lonely and sad in a relationship, you should become social with a network of good friends or people. An individual who has excellent buddies would not be as lonely as somebody who is usually by themselves.

Once again, join a group where you could establish a long-lasting friendship relationship with the right minds.

If you are in a relationship but lonely, and it is truly troubling you, then it is another sign that you should consider professional counseling. The professional counselor could help and provide you with great insights or ideologies on the best ways to better manage your situation of being lonely in a relationship.

Inferentially considering the experience is nothing wrong being alone at times as it happens to all at some points in our lives. It is one of the many things that make us human. Yet, a typical individual would invest some time alone in the course of their life.

Remember, some people get into a relationship just for the sake of not being lonely. Before they knew it, they were caught up in a relationship but still find themselves lonesome.

Consequently, on being deserted, getting into a relationship with someone solely just for the sake of not being alone is truly not a good thing for both parties involved. More so, getting into a relationship with someone just for the sake of not being lonely usually winds up causing problems as the marriage or relationship continues. And another last sad thing about this is that the other partner may not have an idea that you are lonely. Since such understanding is absent, there would eventually be a problem of operating as one. Trying to find the best way to make it work in the situation that you are already married could as well be informing him of the status quo and unity; there could be a permanent solution other than permanent separation.

Step 13 - WAYS TO BUILD EMOTIONAL INTIMACY WITH YOUR PARTNER

What Is Emotional Intimacy and Why It Matters?

Emotional intimacy could be described as allowing yourself to connect more deeply with your partner through actions that convey feelings, weaknesses, and confidence. Part of a relationship is to share your secrets, talk about your relationship and reveal important news for your partner. When both sides can share and appreciate each other's feelings, a couple is generally happier.

Ultimately, emotional intimacy provides a profound sense of security within your relationship, and the freedom to be wholly yourself — warts and everything — without feeling like you're compromising the relationship. A relationship fails in many ways without this intimacy. You may feel cynical or resentful, experience hypersensitivity, have doubts about your partner's commitment to you, or experience feelings of isolation or loneliness, for instance.

Having an intimate relationship without emotional intimacy isn't viable in the long term.

Having an intimate relationship without emotional intimacy isn't viable in the long term. When you think of emotional intimacy as the cornerstone of every relationship, investing your resources (time, money, and energy) in building it and continuing to nurture it, it becomes truly a no-brainer.

WAYS TO IMPROVE EMOTIONAL INTIMACY

Cultivating emotional intimacy is an evolving process and may take some time to master like many things. There are, however, a few things you can do (starting tonight) to strengthen your partner's emotional connection.

1. BE STRATEGICALLY VULNERABLE TO EARN THEIR TRUST

Even if you have spent a tremendous amount of time with someone, breaking down our walls is sometimes hard. Also, if you can't force another to become vulnerable, you can go out of your way to become vulnerable.

Paul Hokemeyer, a psychotherapist, said it is critically important to practice strategic vulnerability. Instead of attempting to become insecure in every area of your life, choose one place to start. This could translate into sharing something that happened at work that you might not have discussed otherwise, expressing a feeling that has been difficult to share in the past, or revealing a fact about yourself that you've been holding on to.

2. GIVE YOUR PARTNER A DAILY AFFIRMATIONS AND COMPLIMENTS

Whether you're in a partnership for six months or 60 years, it's easy to take for granted the positive attributes of our spouse, and sometimes hard to articulate how much we appreciate them.

Making a habit of giving your partner frequent feedback and affirmations will allow you to keep a glimpse of why this person is essential to you and let them know you see them. You never want your partner to feel insignificant because you have failed to express your confidence.

These verbal affirmations are as simple as saying, "I want you to know how deeply I love you" or "I appreciate the time it took you to do x, y, or z."

3. SORT OUT SEXUAL SATISFACTION

A study found that couples reported having a greater emotional connection when they were sexually satisfied. The two are inextricably related, in that sense. Although having sex alone is not a cure-all to strengthen your emotional bond, taking the time to understand and discover the interests of your partner — and having the same reciprocation — will lead to greater feelings of emotional intimacy inside and outside the bedroom.

4. ATTEMPT TO BREAK OUT YOUR DAY TO DAY ROUTINE

With how busy life becomes, it's easy to hit a comfort zone plateau where we push past each other and trying to cross things off our to-do lists. This is in sharp contrast to the beginning of a relationship, where everything we do is fresh and exciting, and then we go beyond and beyond.

This can mean we have lost sight of the importance of doing things for each other that produces the other person's happiness or intimacy. We quit trying to impress, we stop trying to explain, and insecurity and emotions can get lost to the daily routine of this attitude. It is extremely important that we gain time together in a deeper way than just having dinner or bedtime together.

In a relationship, garner motivation from those early courting days. Perhaps you're planning a casual beginner's square-dancing date night; you're choosing to go for ice cream and a stroll, you're turning up with "only because" flower, or you're sitting down together and preparing a weekend getaway.

5. DIVIDE HOUSEHOLD DUTIES EQUALLY

You might be going home for another full-time job after a hard day's work: becoming a mom. "After the kids go to bed, the cleaning is always accompanied by jobs that you have brought home. Intimacy is moved to the side, as a result. If you and your wife both work full time, keeping the household labor division equal and ensuring that one wife doesn't shoulder the entire burden would make you both happier in the bedroom and out.

6. ADD SEX TO YOUR TO-DOS

We schedule appointments for doctors, work meetings, and drinks with friends, so why not sex? It's not the most romantic solution, but with your significant other means setting aside a particular day, you commit to maintaining a healthy sex life. You will feel obligated to hold the appointment this way and will be less likely to make excuses.

7. KEEP THINGS PLAYFUL

Be playful, lighthearted, and tease your partner in a sexy manner. The energy between cat and mouse is a winner. Entice, flirt and get to play hard. Bring out all the ancient sexual energy codes, and let it go. This is a classic instrument and it never fails.

8. MAKE REGULAR EYE CONTACT WITH YOUR PARTNER'S LEFT EYE

The left eye interacts with their right emotional brain. A fascinating study has shown this technique creates trust very quickly and very effectively on a first date. The research behind the appeal of eye contact is pretty interesting. A 2007 study at Aberdeen University found that if they look straight at you and smile, you're more likely to find other people attractive. Making eye contact also makes the expressions more memorable, making you more self-confident and making you honest. Both of which, in creating trust, are beneficial.

Eye contact during interaction diminishes as a relationship progresses over time. To reconnect with your partner more closely, commit to focusing on gazing into each other's eyes while talking. The findings will pleasingly impress you.

9. SHOW GRATITUDE

Consistently telling your partner, "Thank you" will help to strengthen your relationship. "This wonderful virtue goes beyond the protocol and social grace. Simple and sincere thank-you acknowledgments go a long way with your partner. Letting your partner know you're thankful for what they're doing makes them feel like wanted, wanting, and appreciated. "So easy and genuine," Thanks for doing the dishes, babe! ", would certainly go a long way.

10. FIND RANDOM MOMENTS TO REACH AND TOUCH YOUR PARTNER

It can occur anywhere, anytime. For example, you can reach over and caress the back of your partner's head as you drive. You should give them an enormous hug after a long day. It all comes down to the touch. Touching re-unites the mutual emotional connection. It says: I like the way you feel about me, an 'I'm at home with you.

11. BE A GOOD LISTENER

Intentionally put down your phone, put off the TV, shut down the music, and listen to how your partner feels.

Ask follow-up questions such as, how do you feel about that? Can you tell me more? Or something more normal along those lines. This is among the best things you can do for your relationship because active listening shows that you genuinely care for the thoughts, interests, concerns, and dreams of your partners.

12. GET INTIMATE WITH YOURSELF

I mean spiritually and mentally, not sexually.

13. EXPRESSING YOUR LOVE

Intimacy is the nature of your relationship. You can't just talk about love by showing it on a piece of paper or wearing a ring. You need to express love. So if it is essential you want to build intimacy in your relationship, don't leave it on the back burner.

Put energy in there and focus on it. Consider it high on the list of your relationship goals and priorities. Don't let it slip away from your life together.

14. FOREPLAY & SETTING THE MOOD

One idea many sex therapists make use of is making partners schedule sexual time. Anything from cuddling to massages to reading erotic poetry can be a gateway to intercourse that revolves around the engine.

Everybody's style is unique, and as a couple, figure out what works for you — and you should have fun doing that. Notice that each person may experience pleasure in different ways with each progressive stage of physical intimacy and may prefer different stages.

15. REMINISCE

Reminisce on the magnificent times that you had together. When you think about a beautiful experience that you've shared or something amusing that you've experienced, it helps bring you back to that moment because you remember the feelings that surround the occurrence. Recalling pleasurable encounters, you have had, you recapture some of the good feelings linked to those encounters. If you are trying to increase your relationship with your partner, you want to focus on the good memories and what it was like then. Reminiscent of the good interactions helps to keep the emphasis on what's going on in your relationship that can deepen your connection with your partner.

The thing is, you will find all kinds of enjoyable ways to be intimate both in the bedroom and out with your partner. But intimacy at the very heart of it is all about opening up and allowing another person to share in your grandeur and vulnerabilities. If you can't be 100 percent authentically yourself, you're only holding back from knowing what intimacy can offer you in a relationship. True intimacy, all in all, comes from you.

Step 14 - SPICE UP YOUR SEX LIFE

A commitment to unconditional love is the widely accepted description and definition of marriage. This vivid portrayal also captures the underlying driving force of a happy and long-lasting marriage – romance.

Romance is the outward portrayal, expression, and demonstration of love. Therefore, the intensity, frequency, and sustenance are a surefire thermometer to establish the position and strength of your relationship. Romance is also a sure indication of the contentment of partners within a relationship.

In marriage, the traditional expectations of a family driven by culture and conventions are involved in gauging and influencing the relationship. However, romance still retains its crucial role as the glue that nourishes relationships and keeps them going even during rocky times.

In building and sustaining a marriage, there is a need to cultivate oneness and bolster intimacy. You and your partner have to be committed to meet each other's emotional and physical needs. Marriage faces significant dynamism and changes. Marriage partners might fail to hold high levels of commitment at all times. As a result, there is a need for a

Problem-solving approach. When the relationship hits trouble, there is a need for a way to find a solution. In the second or third year of marriage, something typically happens in most marriages. The romantic heat that warmed the

100

relationship before marriage dies down somewhat. The decline of romance leads to a plummeting in the ability of these partners to meet each other's physical and emotional needs. This increases the chances of conflict and the likelihood of divorce or separation. The question here is – how do you guard against the dying passion and fires of romance?

Is there is something about marriages that seems to kill romantic motivation and creativity? At some point in their marriages, couples realize that they no longer take each other to feel the passion, desire, and romance that they once did. In this case, the engagement period sounds exciting to a rather dull workbook. But it does not have to be this way!

There are ways you can re-introduce, utilize, and sustain romance within a married setting. Here are some of the ways to keep the excitement, passion, and heat of love alive within your marriage. This way, it will nourish your relationship with the emotional and physical satisfaction required to you and your spouse happy.

Romance ought to be part of your daily diet

The concept of love, especially in marriage, refers to the unconditional love and robust commitment of the partners to their partners. Romance is essential in a marriage because it is the daily manifestation of this love towards your partner. Romance is the fuel that keeps the marriage engine running. If it dies down, then everything else comes tumbling down.

Keeping romance in your daily diet means deliberately resolving to do romantic things or actions for your partner.

Complement her good looks. For example, for the husband, notice how good she looks, her good mood, how good she smells, and how she makes you feel. Tell her how much you love and desire her body, and how crazy she makes you feel.

Visualizing her and letting her know about how you feel allows her to feel appreciated. It also lets her in on your thoughts, affection, love, appreciation, and attachment to her. It helps keep the romance levels high and maintain the connection you have into the marriage period.

Partners are typically good friends. However, there is a part of your relationship that goes beyond friendship. You share a marriage bed, dreams, and thoughts that are shared with no one else in the world. Therefore, making romance part of your daily interactions helps keep it alive.

This approach also develops it into a good habit to appreciate your partner every day with the same vigor and passion you did before you got married. Such a decision helps marriage through more difficult, challenging, and disruptive circumstances. For example, after the birth of your first child, the relationship and romance might be eclipsed by the attention given to the child and the accompanying chores.

However, making a deliberate effort to focus on your romance at least once a day gives you a fighting chance of maintaining your excitement, passion, and vigor even after transformative events in your lives and relationship.

Aspire and actively seek to meet your partner's romantic needs

Part of your skillset and repertoire should be the ability to learn quickly about your spouse. Within marriages, it means continually learning about your partner through the years and adjusting your approach to suit the moments, circumstances, and periods of your life together. You become a student of your partner to answer the following question – what pleases your partner?

The learning aspect is interesting in marriage because of the gender divide in the perception of romance. Men and women view romance through different lenses. This means that you cannot use your own experience and perspective of passion for making decisions about your partner. Instead, you have to invest time and intimate conversations to establish what works and does not work for your partner.

Honesty plays a crucial role in the learning process. There is a need to be open with your partner regarding your romantic preferences. Feedback is essential to allow your partner to determine whether you like their advances or not. Such frank communications help in building an understanding of each other, which helps bolster the romantic experience for both partners in the marriage.

For example, most men find their romance in physical intimacy. For example, it matters that the female partner "dresses in a sexy way" or "meet me at the door scantily dressed." On the other hand, women typically prefer "to be taken out to a romantic candle-lit restaurant." Others prefer "cuddling in front of the fire" or "spend time talking."

The summation here is that the romantic sense for men is wired to appreciate sight and touch, whereas women want to develop a relationship.

However, meeting your spouse's romantic needs takes more than an understanding of the generic male/female taste differences. It takes a lot more work and focuses on figuring out the specific preferences, needs, wants, and expectations for your partner. When you figure this out, you will be well-positioned to meet your partner's romantic expectations and desires.

Prioritize romance in your relationship

Romance should form a part of the most important and valuable aspects of your schedule. For example, sit down with your spouse and look at your calendars over the next week or two. Find a convenient time for both of you to go out.

Make sure you both write the data down. This will help in building the anticipation towards your day out. The building excitement drives healthy emotions for your relationship and romance.

Moreover, make sure to find time in your calendar for physical intimacy and sex. Typical married couples find no time for sex. When it comes to sex, you should aim for quantity over quality. Without having sex or intimate physical contact regularly, the risk of losing physical connection increases substantially.

The underlying argument supporting the aim for quantity and not quality is that it removes massive expectations for long and technical sessions for lovemaking. Be spontaneous. You can have a quickie in the shower. Or, you can make out like teenagers before you go to bed. The frequency of lovemaking will help build intimate moments that keep the romance alive. And, this can turn into longer lovemaking sessions to everyone's satisfaction.

How you spend your free time matters

Every single day, make a point of spending some quality time with your partner.

How you spend your time contributes significantly towards making you a good husband/wife. You can never be too busy for your partner. Steal a moment or two to check in on him/her, say hello, and whisper sweet nothings into his ear.

Yes, you have to work, and yes, you have other things to do. However, your marriage should never be on the backburner. It should always be at the forefront of what you do.

The mistake most couples do is compartmentalize marriage and romance out of their workplace and workdays. The problem with this approach is that you spend most of the time at work. With marriage removed from the workplace, the time dedicated to your spouse reduces markedly. This makes it harder to maintain the fire of romance when it only makes technical appearances on weekends!

And if your work has to have your absolute attention, find alternative ways of making your partner feel wanted, loved, prioritized, and desired. In this regard, the less time you have available to spend with your partner, the more precious it should be when you are together.

Additionally, when pressed for time, you should make every small moment you have into a pivotal romantic experience. Your marriage will not be like your honeymoon a couple of years after you tied the knot. However, this does not mean that it should be short of mind-bending and genuinely unique moments.

As a married couple, there is a need to learn to make ostensibly small and mundane events or moments into special ones. Moments can be a small as listening to your partner intently and offering your input or help.

Be creative

You should turn your bedroom into a secure, private, erotic, romantic hideaway. It should not be the site for your kids to play, storage for other staff, or a workstation.

Being in the bedroom together should carry an aura of romance, building the sexual tension, heightening the desire and anticipation, and thus keeping heightening the fires of romance.

When your partner calls you and tells you, "I am in the bedroom," it should spark emotions in you connected to your shared time there as well as sexual anticipation.

Creativity also touches on communicating love and commitment to your partner.

Communication is essential to the passing of information from one entity to another party. But in marriage, it takes up a new meaning.

Communicating love is not similar to how you offer a counter-offer to a client. It should be considered and steeped in the history of the relationship you share. It should also be reflective of your knowledge of your partner and nod to the love and romance you share and wish to share in the future.

Communication of love and commitment can involve something as mundane as sitting next to each other at restaurant tables. Taking a seat across from your partner is regarded as more aggressive. This is what you do when you are meeting a potential employer/employee for interviews. Sitting alongside each other allows for some erotic and romantic moments of touch and contact. You can also whisper in his/her ear.

Communication shows intent and communicates love and romance. For example, a mutually practical communication approach within a marriage will schedule room-com date nights. On these nights, each of you can let go. Immerse yourselves in the romance, love, and relationship you share. Moreover, ensure to avoid all the externalities like work or even family. It allows you to escape together and share special moments that are important in keeping your love, passion, and romance alive.

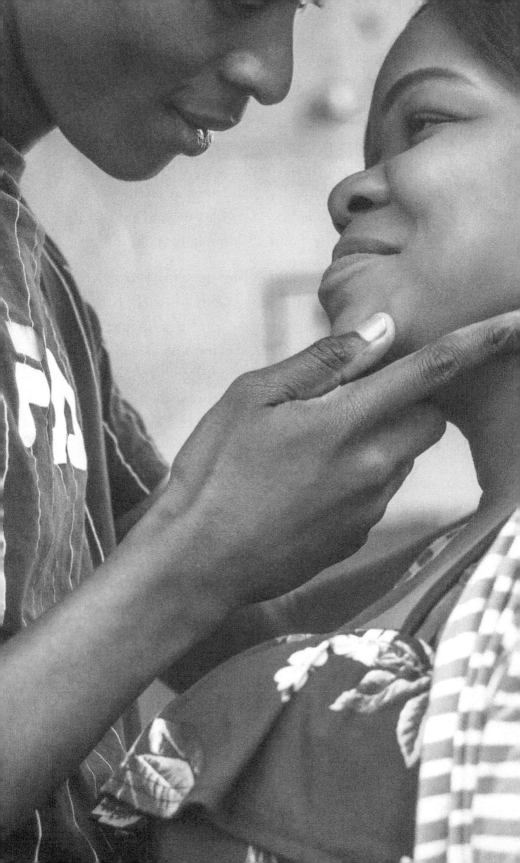

Step 15 - ANALYZING AND ATTACKING ANXIETY

Walk down the street and one in four of the people you pass with either has an anxiety disorder or may encounter one at some stage in their lives. And about half of the people you meet will suffer to one degree or another with anxiety, while they may not have a full-blown anxiety disorder. For several decades the prevalence of anxiety disorders has increased and no end is in sight.

The world is watching in panic, like disasters, terrorism, financial crisis, pandemics, violence, and war endanger a home and family security. Anxiety creates domestic chaos, ruins relationships, creates workers to miss work time, and prevents people from living complete, healthy lives.

Anxiety includes feelings of anxiety, concern, anticipation, and/or fear, and it is the most serious of all the so-called mental disorders. In other words, if you have unnecessary anxiety you certainly aren't alone. And, over the years, numbers have risen. At no time in history have more people been tormented by fear than it is now. Why? For what?

Life has never been as hard as it is now. Workweek grew longer instead of shorter. Broken and mixed families generate increased manageable stresses. Real-time computer screens and tv news carry the latest horrors to your living room. Chronic violence, fighting, and corruption are published in newspapers, forums, tweets, and magazines. Terrorism has traversed the world, rising to new heights.

Unfortunately, as overwhelming as the world today is, only a fraction of people suffering from anxiety are seeking care. This is a concern, as anxiety not only causes emotional pain and depression but also physical strain and even death, as anxiety takes a significant body toll and can even lead to suicide. Anxiety is costing society as a whole, to the rate of billions of dollars.

When people talk about the feeling of anxiety, you can hear any or all of the following descriptions: When my panic attacks start, I feel tightness in my chest. It's as if I sink or suffocate and I start sweating; the anxiety is unbearable. I sound like I'm going to die, and I'm going to have to sit down because I may be sick.

Every day, even on weekends, I wake up with anxiety. I've been worrying all the time, ever since I lost my job. Often I think of going to sleep when it's really bad, and never waking up.

I've had hallucinations and endless images running through my head since my accident about glass shattering, spinning tires, and spinning passengers. I am so irritable and jumpy that I can hardly get through the day.

I'm so afraid of flying that I won't be able to drive, even though I want to.

I'm so concerned about germs and waste that I wash my hands about 30 times a day. I'm just not going to pause.

Anxiety occurs, as you can see, in all sorts of emotions, attitudes, and feelings. When your anxiety starts to interfere with daily life, you need to find ways to ease your anxieties and worries.

Tabulating the Costs of Anxiety

Costs on fear. This affects the sufferer mentally, physically, and financially.

Yet this is not stopping there. Anxiety also puts a psychological burden on everyone.

Stress, worry, and anxiety affect relationships, family, and jobs.

What does anxiety cost you?

Obviously, if you have an anxiety disorder, you'll know the expense of nervous, depressed feelings. Anxiety feels pitiable. You don't have to read a workbook to grasp that. But do you know that in other ways too, untreated anxiety runs up a tab? Higher blood pressure, headaches of stress, and gastrointestinal symptoms can affect your body. Indeed, new studies showed that certain forms of chronic anxiety disorders alter the composition of the structures of the brain.

A toll on your children: parents with anxiety have anxious children more often than not. This is partially due to biology but also because children are learning through observation. Anxious children can be so overwhelmed they won't be able to pay attention in school.

* * * Fat: Anxiety and stress boost the stress hormone called cortisol.

Cortisol allows the abdominal region to store fat, thus increasing the risk of heart disease and stroke. Heat also contributes to eating more.

• More hospital trips: This is because people with anxiety also experience physical signs that are alarming. Besides, anxious people every worry about their health a lot.

• Issues with relationships: People with anxiety sometimes feel irritable. Often they physically withdraw, or do the reverse, and cling to their partners dependently.

Downtime: Missing people with anxiety disorders happens more often than most, usually as a temporary attempt to quench their pain.

Adding up the cost to society

In 2002, UK spent 32 billion pounds (about $53 billion) on mental health services, a large portion of which was spent on anxiety-related issues. Also, countries that spend less on mental health services are incurring significant anxiety disorder costs. These expenses include often decreased productivity — often due to health conditions made worse by anxiety — often Drugs decreased productivity. But the financial loss arising from downtime and treatment expenses does not include the dollars lost to drug abuse, which many of those with anxiety disorders turn to relieve their anxiety. Therefore, anxiety extracts a tremendous toll, directly and indirectly, on both the individual who encounters it and on society at large.

Recognizing the Symptoms of Anxiety

You do not know whether you have an anxiety disorder or an anxiety disorder. This is because there is a wide variety of symptoms involved with anxiety. Every person has a slightly different constellation of those symptoms. And your particular constellation will decide what sort of anxiety disorder you can have.

For now, you should know that, in the form of thoughts or opinions, certain symptoms of anxiety occur. Many symptoms of fear occur in bodily sensations. Many signs often occur in various kinds of nervous behaviors. Many people show symptoms of anxiety in all three forms while others view their anxiety only in one or two places.

Thinking anxiously

People with anxiety usually think differently from the ways others do. If you experience approval addiction, you're probably thinking anxiously: if you're an approval addict, you're concerned a lot about what other people think of you.

•   Thinking in the future and expecting the worst: you think about all that lies ahead and expect the worst possible result as you do so.

•   Magnification: Those who magnify traumatic things are typically more depressed than others.

- Perfectionism: When you are a perfectionist, you believe that every mistake is a complete failure.

- Low concentration: Routinely anxious people report struggling to concentrate their thoughts. Short-term memory often still suffers.

- Running thoughts: thoughts in a current of almost uncontrollable anxiety and concern race through your mind.

Battling Anxiety in Your Relationship

Thoughts have a strong effect on your emotions. Your emotions also affect your thoughts, at the same time. To battle anxiety, you need to be aware of both your thoughts and emotions.

The following true story from our lives shows how profoundly thought affects the way people behave.

We took a cruise some time ago to reward ourselves for having completed a big project. We sat on deck chairs one evening and watched a beautiful sunset: bright red and orange clouds melted into the deep blue sea. Ever so slightly the breeze picked up and the ship rolled gently. We sat comfortably, watching the scene peacefully, and the cradle-like motion. We reflected that we have never felt so at ease in our lifetime.

The weather statement from the captain has disrupted our relaxed state of mind. Apologizing for the inconvenience, he told us he would have to steer a slightly different course because of a storm, and we could feel some choppy seas. Still, he told us there was no danger from the storm.

114

Suddenly the breeze felt a little chilly. The clouds, which had been so magnificent before, seemed sinister. Nervousness was caused by the gentle roll that had relaxed us now. And nothing had changed over the sky or the sea from moments before.

From blissful relaxation to mounting anxiety our minds jerked. We pulled our jacket closer and reflected on how bad the weather looked and maybe we'd be better off indoors.

Apparently, the way we felt influenced our feelings or the way we perceived the weather, a lot. A state of calm happiness turned into anxious fear while the weather hadn't changed by itself.

The goal is to become a detective of thought, capable of uncovering the thoughts that lead to anxious feelings. We're teaching you how to collect facts and put your theories to the test. We help you see how thoughts cause your anxiety all too quickly, and we're giving you validated strategies to turn your nervous thoughts into calm thoughts.

<u>Distinguishing Thoughts from Feelings</u>

Psychologists also interview their clients to find out how they feel about their lives about the latest events. Clients often respond with the way they think of the events rather than the way they feel. Others know how they feel but when it comes to what they think, they are stumped. We address in the next segment why people frequently end up out of contact with their emotions, opinions, or both. Instead, we're exploring how your ideas and emotions can be controlled.

Step 16 - KEEP YOUR PERSONAL SPACE AND LOVE YOURSELF

Love lies at the very center of God's design for all human relationships, whether natural or spiritual. Jesus told us that the two greatest commandments are, first, to "Love the Lord your God with all your heart and with all your soul and with all your mind" (Mt. 22:37), and second, to "Love your neighbor as yourself" (Mt. 22:39b). The two are inseparably linked. God created us not only to receive His love but also to give love back to Him as well as extending it to others. By severing our relationship with God, sin broke the essential "connection" in our ability to give and receive love. Without a vital love relationship with

God it is impossible for us to love either our neighbor or ourselves as we should. When we are confident of God's love for us, however, we can return that love to Him, and that free interchange of love enables us to love ourselves and, in turn, to love others.

Self-hatred is probably the greatest single problem in human society, regardless of culture. Decades of research, study, and experience in the fields of human psychology and behavior have revealed that self-hatred lies at the heart of the vast majority of mental, emotional, and psychological problems. Many people have trouble living with others because they have trouble living with themselves. They find it hard either to give love or to receive love from others because they cannot love themselves.

Unfortunately, the problem of self-hatred is not limited to secular culture or the world of the mentally ill or emotionally unstable. The same plague afflicts many followers of Christ as well. Many of us who are believers have an inferiority complex under which we are constantly putting ourselves down, saying negative things about ourselves, and denying our gifts, talents, and abilities. This sense of inferiority is the product of centuries of teaching in the Church that says it is wrong for us to love ourselves. Such teaching equates self-deprecation with humility when in reality the two are not the same at all. Self-deprecation says, "I am nothing. I am worthless, useless, with nothing of value to give to anyone."

Humility, on the other hand, is simply believing and accepting what God says about us, and God says that we are anything but worthless.

When Jesus said, "Love your neighbor as yourself," He meant that we are to love our neighbor as much as or to the same degree as we love ourselves. Stated another way, we can love our neighbor only to the same extent that we love ourselves. People who do not love themselves cannot truly love anybody else.

Humility is simply believing and accepting what God says about us, and God says that we are anything but worthless.

Please understand that I am not referring to a narcissistic and egoistical self-love that struts around with an inflated opinion of itself while looking down its nose at everybody else. By "loving ourselves" I mean having a positive self-image and a healthy sense of self-worth based on a proper understanding of our place in the love of God and in relationship to God and others.

Why should we love ourselves? What reason do we have? The answer lies in the heart and purpose of God. God created us in His image and likeness, the greatest act and the crowning glory of all His creative work, and He pronounced it "good." Sin marred and distorted that image in us. Nevertheless, we were still so important to God and of such great worth to Him that He sent His Son to pay for our sin on the cross so we could be restored to Him. Through Christ, God recreated us in His image—He remade us, as it were—and again pronounced it "good." We should love ourselves, not in a conceited manner, but simply by accepting for ourselves the value that God Himself places on us.

<u>We Are Accepted by God</u>

One of the first steps in developing healthy self-love is to realize and believe that we are completely and absolutely accepted by God. Paul put it this way in his New Testament letter to the believers in Ephesus:

For He chose us in Him before the creation of the world to be holy and blameless in His sight. In love, He predestined us to be adopted as His sons through Jesus Christ, in accordance with His pleasure and will— to the praise of His glorious grace, which He has freely given us in the

144 Understanding Love: Marriage, Still a Great Idea

One He loves. In Him, we have redemption through His blood, the forgiveness of sins, by the riches of God's grace that He lavished on us with all wisdom and understanding (Ephesians 1:4-8).

Verse 6 in the King James Version reads, "To the praise of the glory of His grace, wherein He hath made us accepted in the Beloved" (emphasis added). Paul is talking here about present reality, not a past experience.

In the past we were unacceptable. Because of our sin, God could not accept us. We were outcasts, separated from Him with no hope on our own of returning to Him. Then Jesus came to earth and died on the cross, taking with Him all the things that made us unacceptable. He bore them in His own body, endured the stain of our sin, was obedient to the point of death, and on the third day rose from the dead. With His blood He washed us clean of our sin, making us pure and holy again.

Then He brought us before His Father and the Father said, "Accepted!"

If God has accepted us, we should be able to accept ourselves. God is not concerned about outward appearances; those don't matter to Him. Regardless of the flaws or defects we may see or imagine in ourselves; God looks at us and says, "I love you. You are accepted. You are beautiful to Me."

God accepts us even with all of our imperfections. Why then do we have such problems with self-acceptance? One reason is the way we perceive our worth, both to ourselves and to others. Many of us may walk around saying, "I'm worthy. God has made me worthy," yet deep inside still feel that we are worthless. We look at our education (or lack of it), our physical appearance, our job skills (or lack of them), our gifts, talents, and abilities (or lack of them) and conclude that we are not worth much.

We will always end up with a false picture of ourselves whenever we evaluate our worth according to criteria that God ignores. Our self-worth has nothing to do with physical tangibles, the standards we usually use to judge our value. God does not look at those things.

The true value of anything is the worth that is placed on it by another. For example, gold is simply a shiny yellow metal, a product of the earth and worthless in itself except for the value that humans place on it. Many people have lusted, fought, killed, and died because of the value they put on gold. In the same way, we need to look not to our standards to measure our value, but to the value placed on us by another—God, our Creator.

LOVING YOURSELF

We will always end up with a false picture of ourselves whenever we evaluate our worth according to criteria that God ignores.

How much are we worth to God? Looking back at Ephesians 1:4-8 we see that God "chose us...before...creation...to be holy and blameless in His sight" (v. 4). "He predestined us to be adopted as His sons through Jesus Christ, in accordance with His pleasure and will" (v. 5).

He "freely" poured out His grace—His unmerited favor—on us (v. 6).

He regarded us as valuable enough to send His precious Son, through whose shed blood we have received "redemption" and "the forgiveness of sins" (v. 7). He did all of this deliberately, out of His own "wisdom and understanding" (v. 8) simply because He wanted to.

We are valuable to God; priceless. We should be careful never to confuse our self-worth, which is given by God, with our appearance, assets, or behavior, or with the behavior or attitudes that others take toward us.

If we make a dumb mistake, we should say, "I made a mistake," not, "I am a mistake." Whenever we fail at something, we should acknowledge, "I failed," but never say, "I am a failure." We should always keep our behavior or performance separate from our sense of self-worth. No matter what happens, no matter how badly we mess up, or how often, we are still worthy and acceptable to God. He has already declared it to be so, and His Word never changes.

Step 17 - THE IMPORTANCE OF BEING ABLE TO MANAGE FAMILY

Family. Let's all let out a collective sigh. What is it about family that we simultaneously yearn for and can't wait to get away from? How can our parents drive us crazy one minute and then make us feel like we belong the next? And how the heck did your partner emerge so normal(ish) from a family like . . . that?

Most of us can say that our family members mean well, but that doesn't mean they don't put enormous strain on a marriage. In this step, we're going to revisit your families of origin by examining your relationships with your parents and your partner's parents. We're also going to consider the role that children play in your marriage, your parenting styles, and how you balance parenthood with partnership. My hope is that you'll finish the chapter with a deeper understanding of your family stressors, and with new strategies for how to deal with them.

Take a moment to fill in the areas of strength and conflict from your everyday issues assessment (here) that will guide your focus in this step.

Revisit Family

Strengths _____ and _____

Conflicts _____ and _____

Family Relationships

In this step, we're going to explore how family relationships are affecting your marriage now. How did you draw your family aquarium? How do your childhood experiences shape your marriage now?

INFLUENCE FROM PARENTS AND IN-LAWS

As we grow up from children to adults, relationships with our parents shift. Let's look at the relationships you have with your parents and in-laws. Many newlyweds and married couples in my practice describe the joys and challenges of staying connected with parents. The following exercises will help you identify your preferences for accepting their influence, the ways their help may come with strings attached, and how fundamental family therapy concepts like relationship triangles and reactivity can help explain the ways family shapes our emotional worlds.

ASSESS YOUR COMFORT LEVEL

Answer True or False to the following statements in parts A and B:

PART A: YOUR PARENTS

T / F I seek guidance from my parents while making decisions.

T / F I care about what my parents think of my choices.

T / F I value time with my parents.

T / FI share personal details with my parents about my life and relationship.

T / FI allow my parents to help me financially.

PART B: YOUR IN-LAWS

T / FI seek out guidance from my in-laws while making decisions.

T / FI care about what my in-laws think of my choices.

T / FI value time with my in-laws.

T / FI share personal details with my in-laws about my life and relationship.

T / F I allow my in-laws to help me financially.

If you answer mostly True (for either part A, part B, or both), you tend to be comfortable accepting influence from your parents and/or from your in-laws. The boundaries are flexible and permeable—information, money, time, and advice flow freely between you.

If you answered mostly False (for either part A, part B, or both), you are not comfortable accepting influence from your parents and/or from your in-laws. The boundaries are rigid and firm—information, money, time, and advice are resisted between you.

COMPARE COMFORT LEVELS

Compare answers with your partner.

Does your comfort level with your parents match your partner's comfort level with your parents (their in-laws) and vice versa? --

Is your comfort level with accepting influence the same for your parents and your in-laws? -----------------------------------

How do similarities or differences between you and your partner strengthen your partnership? How do they cause problems? ---

Where would you like to make changes in accepting more or less influence from your parents and your partner's parents? - --

Were you surprised by your or your partner's answers to the questions in this exercise?

QUID PRO QUOS

The phrase quid pro quo means "this for that." When it comes to parental or family involvement in your lives as a married couple, there are often expectations about what will come in return. These bargains may be explicit, or they may

125

be simply understood. Sure, your mother-in-law is willing to babysit for you, but she expects an invitation to dinner at your house in return. Sure, your father is willing to loan you and your partner money for a car repair, but he expects to be thanked profusely for his generosity.

ARE STRINGS ATTACHED?

Fill in the blanks and discuss with your partner. Here are two examples, from Mei-Lin and Beth, to get you started:

If my --offers help by ---------

---------------------------------, the expectation is that------------------
----

---.

How does this usually go for us?--

If my --- offers help by --

------------------, the expectation is that ----------------------------
----

---.

How does this usually go for us? ----------------------------------
----

RELATIONSHIP TRIANGLES

A relationship triangle is a natural human response to anxiety or conflict in a relationship. When two people feel distant, uncomfortable, angry, or hurt with one another, a third person (or sometimes, a situation, like going to work) gets triangled into balance the emotional intensity. Sometimes that person is within the family system, as a child or parent, and other times that person is outside, like an affair or best friend. Here are a few common examples:

•A husband and wife feel disconnected, and the wife confides in her neighbor.

•A husband and his mother are very close, and the mother shuns the wife.

•A mother and daughter are very close, and the father feels like he has to compete for his wife's attention.

Understanding and identifying triangles within relationships is an advanced skill. Here are detailed examples from Carlos and Janelle and Josh and Heather to help you better understand how triangles operate in family relationships:

DRAW THE TRIANGLES IN YOUR FAMILY

In the space provided, draw a triangle, and on each point, write in the names that make up your relationship triangle.

Draw and label as many triangles as are needed to illustrate all the triangles in your family. What do you notice?

DO SOMETHING DIFFERENT

It's difficult to work to make the changes necessary to rebalance triangled relationships to shift behavior, perspective, and attitudes.

What can you do to shift your position in the triangles in your marriage or family?

----

5 WAYS TO MANAGE IN-LAW INTERFERENCE

1. Communicate clearly, directly, and on time. Don't let problems linger or fester. Don't share concerns with your partner or another family member. And don't beat around the bush—remember, assertive communication is healthy communication!

2. Never put your partner in a position to have to choose between your partnership and their family. Efforts to accommodate your in-laws with respect and kindness strengthen your marriage because they support your partner. Just like it feels good when your partner accommodates your parents (their in-laws), these efforts are reciprocal.

3. Establish boundaries and expectations with your partner ahead of time and stick to them. Decide whether you'll accept loans, how involved the grandparents will be in your parenting decisions, and which family rules can slide when Grandma and Grandpa are visiting.

4. Consider maintaining a "no houseguest" policy. When family members are in town to visit, they stay at a nearby hotel or rental property. Use the time in the morning before they arrive at your house and in the evening after they leave to recharge as a couple.

5. Be yourself. Don't try to meet their expectations of you if it wouldn't be genuine.

REACTIVITY

Many problems in family relationships stem from reactivity or responding to a situation or person with rigid thinking and intense emotions. Reactivity gives us a very narrow lens through which we make assumptions, draw opinions, and observe others. It prevents us from perspective-taking, seeing more than one side of an issue, seeing our part in an issue, and being able to speak and listen from the heart.

Reactivity is an automatic response; like a trigger, it fires quickly. The antidotes to reactivity are thinking, questioning, and pausing, and then speaking from your heart and sharing your values and needs. Asking questions out loud, with genuine curiosity, helps you see the situation within its larger context, allows you to reflect on what has happened, and encourages vulnerability from yourself and others.

IDENTIFY YOUR TRIGGERS

Think about a recent incident when you responded with reactivity or jumped to a conclusion. What were your triggers in that situation?

How did your body react in that situation—with a knot in your stomach or heat traveling up your neck? What did you do to relax and "come down" from that reaction?

Can you imagine another way you could have responded to avoid being reactive?

CHILDREN AND PARENTING

For many couples, parenting children together brings joy and teamwork to the marriage. But for many others, parenting is just another area of disagreement. Whether you are new parents or your children are growing up, let's explore several important dimensions of parenting and how it affects you as a couple.

TRANSITION TO PARENTHOOD

The transition from a marriage of two to a family of three (or more, if you are having multiples) is one of the most difficult for couples to make. You're adding an entirely new set of roles, expectations, behaviors, and experiences to your life—now you're a partner and a parent. One of the hardest parts of this transition can be how gendered it is. Especially for couples today, who tend to prefer egalitarian marriage, the realities of pregnancy, childbirth, and postpartum transform a mostly gender-neutral partnership into rigid slots of "mother" and "father." Let's hear from Carlos and Linda on this topic:

IF YOU ARE NOT YET PARENTS

What are your expectations of what conception, pregnancy, childbirth, and postpartum life will be like?

How do you imagine you'll respond (both individually and as a couple) to infertility, a challenging pregnancy, a birth that doesn't go according to plan, or postpartum depression/anxiety?

132

How will you remain connected as partners through your different roles, gendered or otherwise, during the process of becoming parents?

IF YOU ARE CURRENTLY PARENTS

Were your expectations of conception, pregnancy, childbirth, and postpartum life met, exceeded, or thwarted?

How did you cope (both individually and as a couple) if you encountered infertility, a challenging pregnancy, a birth that didn't go according to plan, or postpartum depression/anxiety?

How did you remain connected as partners through your different roles, gendered or otherwise, during the process of becoming parents?

ATTACHMENT STYLES

Attachment is the idea that all humans—children and adults—need connection and belonging to survive and thrive. As adults, our attachment style influences our vulnerability and our protectiveness. Through attachments with parents, children make meaning of experiences and emotions. Generally, there are three attachment styles:

Anxious: People with anxious attachment are preoccupied with closeness and seek it at all costs. They fear abandonment, they worry they aren't worthy of love, and they set aside their needs to meet the needs of others. I'm not okay without you, so you can't ever leave me.

Avoidant: People with avoidant attachment are disconnected from intimacy and avoid vulnerability. They are quick to find fault in others, they increase the distance to counteract closeness, and they may be perceived as sabotaging relationships. I'm fine without you, so you can leave and I won't care.

Secure: People with secure attachment are comfortably balanced between intimacy and closeness, and independence and distance. They ask for what they need while attending to others' needs, they avoid games or manipulations to maintain relationships, and they accept themselves and others as whole people. I feel safe being close to you; I love you and I love myself.

Differences in attachment styles are a common underpinning of conflict for partners who are also parents. Whether one style resonates more than the others, or you can think of ways you exhibit all three, exploring how attachment affects your marriage is a helpful way to deepen understanding of your—and your partner's—parenting.

EXPLORE ATTACHMENT DIFFERENCES

If you tend to be anxious, can you recognize ways you may be drawn into your children's world to meet your need for closeness at the expense of your partner?

If you tend to be avoidant, can you recognize ways you may abdicate your role as a co-parent to meet your need for independence at the expense of your partner?

How do differences or similarities between your attachment styles contribute to problems in your marriage or your parenting?

PARENTING STYLES

It's not uncommon for partners to parent with different styles. You grew up in different families, and you play different roles in your children's lives. And it's not uncommon for these differences to cause conflict between you. First, let's explore your parenting styles, and then let's learn a communication trick for handling style differences.

The grid in the next exercise has two axes. One is a spectrum of your style of connection to your children, from a warm and nurturing approach to a more neutral and inattentive approach. The other is a spectrum of your style of influencing your children, from fostering autonomy and independence in your child to using authority and control to manage behavior.

EXPLORE STYLE DIFFERENCES

Mark an X within the grid where your parenting style lands now, and have your partner do the same in a different color. Then, mark where your ideal parenting style would be as a couple.

How far away are you from your partner now?

How far away are you now from where you want to be as a couple?

Do your answers surprise you? Are you more similar or more dissimilar than you expected?

MANAGE PARENTING DIFFERENCES

Differences in parenting style often mean differences in parenting behavior. And when these differences cause conflict, the solution is in your communication. So instead of getting frustrated or feeling undermined by your partner, here's a helpful trick: view the situation as if you were watching a foreign film. The subtitles help you understand what the parenting difference means and clues for what to do about it.

The Scene: --

The Action/Dialogue: --
-------------------------------- sees/hears: ----------------------
----

The Subtitles: Partner 1: ---------------------------------------
----

The Subtitles: Partner 2: ---------------------------------------

----

The Resolution: --

How does awareness of the subtitles help you understand your partner's parenting choices?

How does this awareness help you decide as a team how to resolve differences in your approach?

KEEPING MARRIAGE, A PRIORITY

On an airplane, you are always advised to put your own oxygen mask on before helping your child put on theirs. This is a good analogy for why you must keep your marriage a priority over the children. Your marriage "mask" goes on first so you can respond well as a team to your children's needs. This means prioritizing date nights, taking some child-free vacations, and remembering that you are a partner at the same time that you're a parent.

ASSESS PRIORITIES

In the midst of parenting demands, how well are you doing with keeping your marriage a priority?

In what ways do your children currently come before your marriage?

What are you modeling for your children concerning where your marriage falls on your priority list?

Step 18 - NO MORE FIGHTING

Romantic relationships are some of the most intense emotional attachments we create in our adult lives, and they make us feel all kinds of ways that don't make it into quaint quotations in Hallmark cards.

Even on your way to "no more fighting," you will have moments when you criticize each other, bicker, and get irritable. Both of you, at different times, will be self-absorbed or show a lack of sensitivity. Realistic communication is imperfect. Falling short of our goals in the process of closing the gap between where we are and where we want to be is part of learning new skills. When fights happen, don't let them stop you from recalling your overarching intention. Stay true to habits and practices that reduce unproductive conflicts and strengthen your bond.

I get this question a lot from couples: "We know how to try to prevent fights, and we know how to make up, but what do we do right smack in the white-hot center of a scary, hurtful argument?"

Here are 10 actions you can take so no more fighting can take place in your relationship:

1. Recognize your relationship horror stories.

2. Recognize you're in the middle of a fight. This can allow you to switch gears and know that something needs to be done differently and consciously now.

3. Bring your "true adult" into play. Resist resorting to your "pseudo-adult strategies." Soothe your own "inner orphan."

4. Remind yourself you do have options even if things feel temporarily hopeless.

5. Practice "holding your relationship in high regard." This is one of five skills outlined by the founder of the Relational Life Institute, Terry Real. This means thinking positively about your relationship even when it feels anything but positive. Remind yourself that this moment is temporary and it doesn't define your relationship.

6. Use the Imago Dialogue with your partner, mirroring, validating, or empathizing. Take psychological ownership for some small part of what's happening between you.

7. If nothing you're doing helps, and your partner is still triggered, tell them you want to keep things emotionally safe between you by taking a brief time-out. You will come back in 15 or 20 minutes and try to address the issue when you feel more centered.

8. Do a re-do. Restart the "scene" of your disconnection a moment or two before the trigger point and redo it more consciously and kindly.

9. Try a one-minute Vent Box. Only use this mid-fight if your partner agrees and feels comfortable opening a Vent Box for you, and only if you can direct your

frustration at the situation rather than at your partner. Venting at your partner mid-fight will only escalate it.

10. Use a Love Ritual on the spot, like a Feeling Check-in or an appreciation.

When couples fight, it can feel like a tropical storm. Reactivity can bring down lines of communication and leave obstacles behind that block connection. If you are in a relationship where your arguments escalate, you know that fights can come on unpredictably, and strong. The frustration of arguing with your partner can leave you feeling hopeless over time. It's defeating. Without a connection to the intimacy that brought you together, a relationship can feel empty and really, really lonely.

DEALING WITH ANGER IN MARRIAGE

Recognize anger

Were you upset before and when you were asked "what happened", saying "no mistakes"? Most of the time, the husband/wife tries to hide their anger to avoid solving a specific problem. In other cases, husbands do not feel they have the right to be angry and therefore do not pass on their feelings to their husbands. It's okay when you're angry, and it's okay to tell your husband how you feel. From time to time he gets angry normally. Better to leave it with love than to block it.

Understand what you are angry about

Often due to the fragility of relationships between people, they misunderstand the words or actions of the husband. There are times when expectations are not met due to a lack or limitation of what, when, or how something should be done. Due to the lack of clarity or anger in the contacts, a fight begins. Before you get angry, be sure to give your husband the benefit of the doubt.

Agree to stop verbal or physical explosions

Attacking each other is not only unhealthy and dangerous but also inappropriate for a couple who claim to love each other. It is strange that a husband can annoy his wife without closing his eyes, but if someone else does not respect his wife, he will be ready to hit the man on the head. How does this husband who has the right to show anger in marriage feel?

One way to break this habit is to make the couple agree that as soon as the discussion turns into a verbal or physical breaking point, one of them will leave. If necessary, leave the door and around the corner or to the neighbors' house, if that's what is needed to calm the situation.

If you are dealing with anger in a marriage, you can overcome it with a small obligation to understand the root cause, discuss it constructively, and agree not to let anger break the bond between you.

Often all you need is a little paperwork and a court visit. This sad reality is likely to help many people end their marriage before they try to save them. If you are thinking of getting divorced, you need to take some time and try to restore a healthy marriage. Although the process is simple, divorce is not a decision that should be made easily.

There is no single model that leads to the end of the marriage - in fact, there are many different processes, such as unique couples. Regardless of whether your marriage includes high-profile fights, negative chipping, or total avoidance, you need to find a safe way to communicate with another cone if you want to restore a healthy marriage. There can be no reconciliation without communication. In this regard, couples who feel comfortable in combat can have an advantage over those who completely avoid their problems.

These silent partners may have to learn to accept conflicts before they can solve their problems.

We propose that the ability to express our needs and problems without fear of reprisals and the ability to think about our partner's needs objectively is very important for the restoration of a healthy marriage - a position supported by Dr. John Gutman, a researcher in the laboratory of love. Avoiding problems is the main cause of a failed relationship.

If communication is the key to trying to restore a healthy marriage, it is important to learn to communicate clearly and without fear. To this end, here are some useful tips to help you work in marriage:

Take the time. As our lives and relationships develop, it is very common for a couple to focus on each other for professional, family, and personal interests. The key to your efforts to restore a healthy marriage is to devote time to teamwork, sharing experiences, and communication. Even if you spend one night a week playing a board game, this time it isn't full of kids, television, bills, and other distractions.

Start listening. It's amazing how easy it was to get our partner's ideas and opinions back, and we really couldn't listen. By publishing a magazine, turning off the TV, or turning it off while talking to our partner, we get valuable information about their life, letting them know that we appreciate what they say.

Don't accept hypotheses. Is your partner acting detached? Is it clear that something disturbs them? Don't think you're a problem and start fighting before you understand what's going on. Maybe someone at work rubbed them badly, or it might only take a few minutes of quiet time to regroup. Despite this, hypotheses can be a serious problem. Work to get to the bottom of the topic and work from there.

Walk in their shoes. Especially when both partners work full time and lead active lives, some husbands may seem to be just two ships that survive the night. Set a point to find out what's going on in the life of your business partner and his family and friends. Participating in their lives outside of total time will help you anticipate their busy times and avoid friction before it starts.

Leave your judgment outside the door. People process information and pressure in several ways. One person may need to breathe the ferry by going to a party with friends, while the other person can recharge their batteries by resting in a quiet room with a good book. Your partner's needs may not meet your needs in any case. By listening to their needs and interests, without judging or criticizing what they say, it is possible to restore a healthy marriage.

Marriage is not easy - nobody says so. If you sincerely wish to work to restore a healthy marriage, it may not be too late. The conflict may be related to communication and some may find it very difficult to manage, but it is a step in the right direction. Don't be afraid to rely on expert skills to assist you in this complex but useful process.

Sometimes relationships can be difficult, on which it is necessary to work constantly individually and in pairs. However, no matter how difficult it is, remember that it can also be very useful. Download my free e-book and videos and find out what steps you need to take to restore my ex. If you use these resources, I think you will see that they will help you restore the couple.

CONCLUSION

Thanks for making it through to the end of this workbook. I hope it was informative, and the workbook was able to provide you with a lot of tools you need to achieve your goals whatever they may be.

The importance of communication in marriage cannot be overemphasized as it affects other aspects of our lives and improves productivity at work. Married couples that want to live a happy life should practice things that enhance bonding with their partner. You should also be wary of some red flags mentioned in this workbook that could hamper the cordial and romantic relationship that exists with your spouse.

The next step is to apply everything that you have learned and have a happier marriage. The techniques in this workbook take practice for you to really learn them, and for you to be able to apply them effectively. Feel free to review these techniques and even modify them. Also, take note that communication is an art. As such, feel free to device your technique that can help further improve your communication with your spouse. You may have to do make trial and error to identify the ones that work, as well as those that fail to make any positive impression.

Also, note that building a lasting marriage takes continuous effort and one should be intentional about making the communication between both parties work. It takes time, effort, and dedication to enhance communication between spouses, but it's a worthy investment to make. Don't be discouraged if it doesn't happen in an instant; keep trying and keep communicating until you reach a level of mutual understanding. Attaining a level of mutual understanding should be your primary goal while you build on the success achieved from improved communication.

I would also like to congratulate you because just the fact that you have reached this part of the workbook only goes to show that you truly value your relationship. In a relationship, especially in marriage, you really have to support each other now and then. If communication is one of the things that your spouse is not very good at, then you should cover that part for him or her.

The simple fact that you're reading this workbook means that you are doing your duty so well as the spouse. Remember not to give up on your marriage. By learning to communicate more effectively with your spouse, you will be able to experience a big improvement in your marriage. It's also an effective way to bring the fire of intimacy back into your marriage.

Marriage is sacred and learning to communicate effectively with your spouse can both save a marriage from falling apart and can help you create a wonderful and happier marriage. If you truly love your spouse, then do not give up on him or her. Keep working on your communication techniques and keep trying. Do everything that you can to make your marriage work.

It is not really difficult to improve the level of communication in marriage. By now you should already know the specific things that you need to do when you engage in a conversation with your spouse. You may not be able to notice the improvements right away, but you will definitely notice them over time. This workbook is not just about communication; it is a workbook about connection and love, and it teaches you to love your spouse with all your heart, mind, and soul.

BOOK 2

Ellie Edwards - Nolan Sanders

A COUPLE'S DEVOTIONAL

Our Journey with God

A year of devotions for married couples.
52 weekly scripture-based reflections to nurture
your relationship and grow together in faith.

TABLE OF CONTENTS

Introduction

Week 1: Know Each Other

Week 2: Respect Each Other

Week 3: Flexibility

Week 4: Confidence

Week 5: Emotional Needs and Resources

Week 6: Spirituality

Week 7: Intimacy

Week 8: Learn To Communicate Always

Week 9: Resolve Conflicts

Week 10: The Small Stuff

Week 11: To Grow the Relationship

Week 12: To Forgive

Week 13: Always Help Each Other In Difficulties

Week 14: Always Keep the Relationship Lively

Week 15: Smile and Play Together

Week 16: Gratitude

Week 17: Give And Receive Love

Week 18: Financial Planning And Decision-Making: What Are Your Habits?

Week 19: Listen To One Another

Week 20: The Spice of Appreciation

Week 21: Steer Clear Of the Desires of the Body

Week 22: Reconciliation over Retaliation

Week 23: Protect the Sanctity of Marriage

Week 24: Affirmation That Strengthens

Week 25: Learning Each Other's Language

Week 26: The Comparison Trap

Week 27: Open And Honest Discussions

Week 28: Sacred Roles to Play

Week 29: Handling Frustration in Marriage

Week 30: Build Your Marriage on the Positives

Week 31: Marriage Is Holy, Treat It As Such

Week 32: Intellectual

Week 33: Interdependence

Week 34: Don't Compete, Coordinate

Week 35: Creating Habits

Week 36: Parenting Together

Week 37: Loving Without Limits

Week 38: Spend Some Time Together

Week 39: Remember Holiness and Purity

Week 40: Laying the Perfect Foundation

Week 41: True Generosity

Week 42: Think Before You Respond

Week 43: Keep your Word

Week 44: Anxiety in Relationship

Week 45: Confidentiality

Week 46: God Should Be the Center

Week 47: Equality over Inequality

Week 48: Set Relationship Goals

Week 49: Money and Finances

Week 50: Physical Intimacy

Week 51: Alone Time Matters

Week 52: God Is Always With Us

Conclusion

INTRODUCTION

So often in relationships, the difficult conversations, hard decisions, fun times, and dates end up happening spontaneously, end up getting shoved into one of the times when one or both of you are fried and ready to climb into bed. Decide to start doing that differently by taking some time and discovering what your rhythms are. Commit to giving each other more of the best of each other and the cleaning of the house less of it.

While I'm sure that you, like us, have an unwavering love for God in your heart, many of us wait to begin an urgent conversation with him until the going gets tough. But if we don't regularly reflect on the incredible things God has done for us, we risk only turning to him when we want an escape route from our troubles. By comprehending his caring and generous nature daily, and regularly praising him for it, we are more likely to remain hopeful when we inevitably face situations that challenge our faith. If we can cultivate closeness in times of plenty, imagine how much more powerful our connection with him will be in times of turmoil. Indeed, adopting a steadfast attitude of gratitude is invaluable to helping us cope with everything from everyday disappointments to physical and spiritual crises.

In this devotional book, you will learn the right way to be in love as a Christian and the proper channels that you should use. In the same light, you will get insightful verses from the holy book that should guide you in your journey of keeping your matrimony holy and living within the confines and the comfort of the highest.

As a Christian, you always need to be on the same page with your father in heaven. Every little thing you do should make him happy and reflect his image. This applies even when it comes to Love. Whether it is courtship, engagement or marriage, you will need to make sure it is done to God's high standards. This devotional is designed to help you achieve exactly that. You can achieve more from it if you use it in these steps.

Over the next one year, each week will have a topic of focus supported by a verse from the bible. Your intention should be to read the verse, internalize it and regurgitate. It would help if you would try and identify how that particular verse applies to your life. That way, it has more meaning.

After the verse, there is a brief interpretation, short story or analogy that helps to make the verse easy to understand and digest. This is a great resource if you need better understanding or in depth understanding of the days verse. It also helps you prepare for the next part which is equally important in your daily communion with God.

As usual, you will need to ask God for guidance in your marriage as a couple or for the stage that your relationship could be in. Each week has a prayer that has been specially designed with regards to the theme of the week. You can feel free to recite the prayers that have been formulated or, you can easily come up with your own. Better yet, you can recite one in the book and extend it with one of your own.

We are Ellie and Nolan, a married couple for more than twenty years. We are already in 40s. 45 years old and 48 years old to be exact. We have studied couple psychology and therapy for years. We experiment every day with ourselves with what is written in the book. We have helped many couples of friends and relatives over the years to find the right way to a long and peaceful couple life.

Enjoy your Love Journey

1 Thessalonians 5:11

"Therefore encourage one another and build one another up, just as you are doing."

Doing things together helps bring you closer. Remember when you were dating you always looked forward to spend time together and enjoy each other's company. Probably commitments weren't as demanding as they are now but you still need to find time to do stuff together. Any activity will be useful especially if both of you enjoy it. Couples who spend time together solve their issues more amicably since they are close and hence understand each other better. They get to communicate more and thus, areas of conflict are averted or solved early enough.

Humans crave to touch and get physically close with these people they love. Married people need to be as physically close in many instances as possible. Holding hands, hugging, kissing sitting close together, eye contacts, massaging each other are various ways in which to achieve this. In marriage, these small acts of closeness often are not present. To rekindle your love, you need to reestablish these with your partner. Just grab any opportunity to be physically close to them whether in public or private. They will work wonders in your marriage. When we feel emotionally close to someone, we love them more and get to share even our most intimate thoughts that lead to a stronger bond.

With time, couples can find themselves emotionally distance from their partners. They do not share their feelings and simply no longer understand each other as they used to. It's something we need to practice a lot. We get to open to each other about all aspects of our lives. Your spouse should be the first person with whom you discuss about anything happening in your life. If you ever find yourself going to someone else and keeping your spouse out of other things, then, there's a problem and both of you need to work on it. I know it sounds a bit off but emotional closeness is something that lacks in our marriages and hence the many conflicts we face. If he comes over to your vine and you do get to feel right, be in control, be validated, be rescued, or feel like you're winning, it's not the garden or your relationship that ultimately wins – it's the parts of you that feel needy, unsure, wounded, scared, or worthless that do.

Let's say that the climbing vine you want him to tend with you is about how you don't feel supported to grow and invest in your business dreams. You have a vision of a beautiful flowering vine that climbs up the trellis and emits the most delicious of scents. When it blooms, it blooms with cash and abundance and supports your family's Money Tree. But to go for it, you have to rip up the ugly, bug-eaten one that's currently climbing that same trellis. You want your partner to quit pruning that damn tree over there and join you. You're crushed that he can't see the vision you hold for this sweet-smelling future and feel so let down by his lack of support that you're yelling at him across the garden about how dumb it is that he can't see how strong you are and how fantastic this business will be and how you're so unhappy that he's not here with you.

Meanwhile he's over at the Money Tree pruning it, fertilizing it, and putting in effort to have it grow more cash so he can ensure that your finances stay stable while you are over there renovating that climbing vine. He knows you're strong, capable, and ready to achieve your vision. That's why he's happy to leave you to do it alone while he handles the stuff over here. He's shouting at you to listen to him about how he is supporting you and telling you exactly what he's doing over here by the Money Tree to give you and him some breathing room. He's feeling annoyed at having his motivations questioned all the time and is getting angry that you can't trust him to do something on his own that will benefit the family.

Neither of you is hearing the other. Communication is happening but you're speaking different frequencies. He's hearing the strong you and pushing back against the needy you who want his approval and wants him to do some of the work because you're scared, you'll fail and fall on your face. You're hearing the provider in him but pushing back against the fears he has about money and not having enough.

Both of you see the vision and believe in it but allow the needy scared parts of you to run the show. No one ends up winning, and the disconnect only deepens.

Solution? Know that you don't have to agree on or even fully understand your partner's viewpoint to be able change the energy and find a solution that works for you both. But you do have to listen deeply and hear where he's coming from.

Maybe he stays over there and tackles the Money Tree solo to give you breathing room for your business vine. Maybe you go to him and help him with the Money Tree for a while, and then you both go over to the vine to help it grow and flourish. Maybe you realize that you both want the same thing and decide that this isn't a relationship hotspot after all. You do your work to soothe the needy, scared parts of each of you so that all the abundance-providing plants can grow and thrive.

Take the areas of your garden that you indicated as hotspots, and take some time to answer the questions below about them.

1. In as few words as possible, what is going on to cause the hotspot(s)?

2. What does your partner believe is going on to cause the hotspot(s)?

3. What have you tried to do to fix this?

4. Knowing what you know now about your relationship as a garden, what are you willing to try that's different from what you've tried before?

Don't fret if your answer to question number 4 is that you're not sure. There's a lot of book left. You'll get there.

Balance

Nature has rhythms and balance. Your Relationship Garden has rhythms and balance.

Balance is essential in your garden, much as it is in nature. Too much heat and sunshine leaves you depleted and parched for rain and rest. Too much rain and the garden floods. Too many pests and the plants die. Too much of a single nutrient and problems occur. You need balance to be able to bloom and grow. The right amount of light and dark, adulting and playtime, sexy time and quiet, lazy times, busyness and slowness.

The tricky thing with balance is that is can look like you need one thing when you need another. A garden that's been heavy on the money stress and to-do lists can make it seem like what needs to happen is making more money and getting to the bottom of the to-do list, when really, you both need rest and rejuvenation. You need to do less, not more.

A relationship that's feeling disconnected needs more intimacy, touch, and presence instead of giving in to feelings of frustration, anger, and resentment that only feed more disconnection.

What needs to happen to come back into balance can feel counterintuitive and strange. It will take you out of your comfort zone. Let it.

Think of it like a porch swing that has been locked into a pattern of only going forward for months or years. It's going to feel off-putting and strange to begin to swing backwards as well as forward. It might even make you a little nauseous, like you want to grab onto the arm of the swing and hold on for dear life. It might even give you butterflies as your body re-learns how to be in a rediscovered kind of motion. That's how you know you're coming back into balance. Learn to know and love that feeling of disorientation. Heck, you might even start to fall in love with it and call it by its real name: exhilaration.

(Kind of like the feeling of falling in love, yes?)

What in your garden feels out of balance?

Rhythms

Along with balance, your garden has rhythms and seasons. You both have rhythms each day, week, month, and year as well. Each day has light and dark, and each week has warm days and days with crappy weather. Each month has low points and high points, and each year has seasons of growth, harvest, and rest.

168

Each year, you have seasons that you like best and in which you feel most productive. You have times of the month that are low-energy and times that are higher energy. Same with weeks – you have days during the week when you can get stuff done and days you want to do nothing, no matter how rested you feel or how light your garden work for the day. Even each day can be broken up with times of motivation and times of wanting to rest. Times when you have no energy and times when you have lots.

Your relationship is the same. You and your partner will end up syncing up a bit, but not all the time. You might be a night owl, and he might be an early riser. He might love Mondays and is ready to roll, while you're not high in energy until Wednesday.

You might feel like resting more during your period and have more energy a couple weeks later. He might feel low at the beginning of the month and be fine the rest of the month (men have hormone cycles too). You might love spring and summer, and he might prefer the colder months of fall and winter.

The point? If you're in entirely different cycles and rhythms, you're going to have a hard time having energy to do the things he wants to do when he wants to do them, and vice versa. It might take some digging to find the energy for romance in the bedroom if he's a morning lover and you're a take-me-late-at-night-by-moonlight kind of a gal.

There's also a tendency to save your relationship gardening for a low-energy day, choosing to accomplish more work and home stuff when you're at your most energetic instead.

Begin to track your rhythms. Not only the higher and lower energy point of the days, week, and month, but also when you feel the most amorous and frisky on a weekly or monthly basis. Track what happens with your menstruation cycles and with the seasons.

If your high-energy day is Wednesday, plan a date night or time together on a Wednesday and feel the small transformation when you're giving him a non-exhausted part of your time and attention. See how the subtle energy shifts when you have conversations when his energy is higher, and you still have energy to think and contribute in meaningful ways.

If you give your garden more of your sexy energy, you'll get enjoy the warm glow of a happy garden rippling out to other areas of your life.

It's time to begin to honor the rhythms of nature and watch the magic happen.

Acceptance

There is something powerful and courageous about being able to state out loud to yourself clearly, or anyone you feel safe sharing with, precisely what's going on with your relationship without shame. I'm talking about the good, the bad, and the ugly.

Acceptance of where you are and what's going on is the first step in changing the energy in the garden. You can't clear it, yank out the deeply rooted weeds, or re-plant anything if you don't see what's at the heart of it all.

1 Peter 2:17 ESV

"Honor everyone. Love the brotherhood. Fear God. Honor the emperor."

Do you remember the comedian who used to say, "I just don't get any respect"? We laughed about it, but how many people really know what respect is? Dictionaries say "respect" means to feel or show honor or esteem for a person, to hold them in high regard, to treat with deference, to show consideration for. In marriage, respect means you notice things about your partner that no one else does. God's Word calls you to love one another as you love yourself and to respect each other.

Will you have a respectful marriage? This is part of our calling as believers. The Scripture passage for today instructs both husbands and wives to respond to one another with respect. Do you understand what that means in marriage?

Consider the following questions as you evaluate your respect for one another now and in the future:

• In a tense situation, do I cut off my partner when he or she holds a view different from mine?

• When I think my partner is wrong, do I become offensive and harsh trying to put him or her in place?

• In trying to get a point across, am I gently persuasive or opinionated and demanding?

• Am I driven so much by the need to be right that I try to pressure my spouse into my position? Do I intimidate my partner?

• Do I ever interrupt my partner when he or she takes too long to respond?

• Do I ever put my partner down in public or make fun of him or her so that it hurts?

• Do I get irritated because my partner's thinking or communication style is different from my own?

Yes, these are questions that meddle. But answering them is a good step toward building a respectful marriage. As one author said, respect begins when we "learn to practice careful listening rather than threatened opposition, honest expression rather than resentment, flexibility rather than rigidity, loving censure rather than harsh coercion, encouragement rather than intimidation."

Sincere respect creates space for your partner to develop individuality and potential. It creates rather than restricts freedom. How will the respect be in your marriage relationship?

WEEK 3: FLEXIBILITY

Philippians 4:12-14

"I know how to be brought low, and I know how to abound. In any and every circumstance, I have learned the secret of facing plenty and hunger, abundance and need. I can do all things through him who strengthens me. Yet it was kind of you to share my trouble."

No matter how well you know your spouse before marriage, there are surprises. There the well-known story of the young wife who carefully trimmed the edges off the roast before placing it in the roasting pan. When her husband asked her why she did this, she replied, "Mother always did it." When the young couple asked the bride's mother why she trimmed the roast, that good woman explained, "To make it fit the pan. I only had one baking dish, and it was usually not large enough for a roast."

Families develop traditions, and those of one partner might not be the same as those for the other. Some families open Christmas packages on Christmas Eve, and save stockings for Christmas morning, for example. Some put up decorations right after Thanksgiving Day, while others wait until the night before so that the youngsters go to sleep in an ordinary house and wake up to Wonderland. While these things somewhat fit into the "small stuff" category, they can sometimes be overwhelmingly important – especially in those first years when moving into the marital home might mean the first year ever away from the childhood home.

Communication, trust and love are essential in figuring out how to blend traditions, customs and methods of working together; but both sides are going to have to develop a degree of flexibility. Perhaps one partner just isn't comfortable with opening all the gifts on Christmas Eve, but the other one will have a hard time adjusting to the idea of waiting until Christmas morning. Perhaps they might each open one gift the night before and save the others for the following day.

The solutions to such difficulties – and they can become significant difficulties if not discussed and attended to, because such things have that aura of "home" and "security" about them – are not as important as the process of discussing them calmly with loving tenderness, and each partner developing a solution with which he or she can live.

After a few years, that solution might very well become a cherished tradition.

Speaking of cherished traditions and flexibility, one area that couples are most likely to have to develop their own style and solutions is in the bedroom. While youngsters might have seen their parents kiss, and they probably saw them working together, an adequately closed door precludes sharing adult relationships – and appropriately so. Therefore, much of what a young couple might know about sex might come from paperback novels or popular sex manuals. For the basic mechanics, these are usually more than sufficient.

What they might not be prepared for is that every intimate moment does not have to be awesome. Indeed, there should be some fantastic moments; but there are other moments, as well. These might include a sleepy, tired quicky and then cuddling until you both fall asleep, or a gentle affirmation that you are both alive and still trying.

Tired can grow to dominate your primary response to just about everything as you grow older and have more responsibilities. Make time for each other. Send the children to the grandparents for one night, and indulge in a candlelight dinner – even if it is just vegetarian spaghetti. Plan a day where you can both take off from work (flexible vacation days are good for this one) and spend the day together – at home – while the kids are at school or at camp. Call a moratorium on discussing troubling parts of your lives – such as how you are going to come up with the funds for the vehicle insurance – and focus just on each other. Building a relationship is a skill, and like all skills, it needs practice. In order to get in that practice, you need to make time to spend together.

Proverbs 3:26

"For the Lord will be your confidence and will keep your foot from being caught."

Trust is perhaps the most fundamental and yet essential element in a successful relationship. Only when we are able to trust our partner fully and can they trust us can we truly be safe and happy. The magic is that TV and films tell us that we must have when predictability, routine, and things with which we can count are, in fact, much more important to the health of the relation. The following seven suggestions will help you to identify if your relationship is good and how your relationship can be successful if not. The following are seven steps to build confidence in a relationship.

Consistency is the first thing to look for. In your relationship, how honest are you? Your friend, how about it? Can you count on each other? Are you there regularly every day for each other? Romance and excitement are beautiful decorations, but daily routine and reasonable standards lead to a sense of security. Being reliable every day will build a trust-based relationship.

The next thing you have to be careful is communication skills. How well do you send your intended message to and from your partner? Do your words correspond to your facial expressions? Does the language of your bodysuit what you say? Is your intended message sent, too? Many contradictions in a relationship result from a misunderstanding. This is not the toothpaste cap; it is usually a communication malfunction at the base. You and your partner must be able to trust each other's words, to be absolutely sure of what is said. If your words suit your body language, you can build confidence in a relationship.

Believing in yourself, believing in your partner and in the competence of each other as people is essential to a trust-built relationship. If your partner has things with which you are not confident, a gentle and frank discussion on your insecurities is much better than silence, anger, and frustration to build a relationship of confidence. Seeing the qualities of your partner and then feeling complimented and appreciated creates a feeling of comfort and acceptance. This will come back to you in effect. If your partner does anything that you don't like or are unable to do, a caring and supportive conversation will become the foundation of a loving and trusting partnership, although it is sometimes challenging.

In any successful relationship, complete honesty is imperative. The fourth step you will take is to learn how to be loyal to your partner. You can't build confidence in a relationship if you keep secrets. Any kind of secrecy would kill the trust in a relationship. It can seem basic and straightforward to be honest and open, but it takes purpose. The truth is always revealed, and the truth always frees you. Keeping a secret barrier, you and your partner. Secrets need the energy to maintain and more lies to maintain. It is time and energy that you can put into your relationship. Regardless of how difficult it seems, an honest and open relationship is always a trustworthy one.

Good communications are a necessary part of building confidence in a relationship already identified, but the fifth step, which brings your needs to the next level. It can be uncomfortable, especially early in a relationship, to share your needs. Yet we meet our needs whether or not we

176

communicate them and often unhealthily. To maintain a solid relationship and build confidence, your physical, emotional, and social needs need to be shared with your partner. You must also be willing to hear and try to meet the needs of your partner. Having your girlfriend or boyfriend feels what you need or are upset creates tension and frustration in building trusts in a connection. Expressing your desires doesn't make you selfish, but self-aware, and you can trust your partner a great deal.

Step 6 is learning to say no. It is of human nature to like people, but if you put the need for others and want them forward, it can always have a negative effect. If you say yes or no, then you give a confusing message that makes your partner unhappy. He/she must know what you're saying. It's a good thing if your partner voices his wishes, but you don't have to say yes to it all. Tell no when you have to make your partner see who you are and appreciate you when you set limits. If you never say no, a partner cannot respect you. Standing down and seeing your partner do the same creates a climate of giving and taking, when appropriate, and helps build trust in a relationship.

Step No. 7 is all about you. As a human being, you must always continue to grow and extend. Anything that is alive requires constant care and attention and continues to grow and change. By continuously improving yourself and allowing your partner to do the same, you will become two stronger halves of your relationship. You must also maintain the relationship constantly as your own living being apart from both of you. Like a river, sometimes the water slows down and becomes dull. This enlarges and slows, the bottom vanishes. Eventually, the river is narrow and chaotic to maintain health. The water flows across rocks and drops down the cascades. The bond will be the same, and while the rough sections can be painful, after a waterfall, the cleanest water comes. Recognizing and coping with these facets of a relationship can build trust in a relationship.

WEEK 5: EMOTIONAL NEEDS AND RESOURCES

Revelation 22:18-19

"I warn everyone who hears the words of the prophecy of this book: if anyone adds to them, God will add to him the plagues described in this book, and if anyone takes away from the words of the book of this prophecy, God will take away his share in the tree of life and in the holy city, which are described in this book."

A relationship doesn't happen in a vacuum, so when things are going wrong, you also need to have a good look at what else is happening around you.

How balanced is your own life? How balanced is your partner's life? What other things are impacting on your relationship? What essential needs are being met or not being met for you both? What are your stressors? Are they permanent or temporary? What can you do to alleviate them?

Everyone knows that, as human beings, we all have physical needs, for example for water, food, and oxygen. What is less well-known is that we also have emotional needs, such as a need for safety and security, emotional connection, meaning, and belonging.

When our emotional needs are not sufficiently met, we can become emotionally ill, with stress, anxiety, or depression. If

178

our emotional needs are met well, particularly if each need is met through multiple sources, we will be more resilient to lives many stressors and challenges.

In a relationship, obviously both people's needs are important. If someone is very unhappy, stressed or anxious, it is very likely that at least one of their essential needs is not being met. When that is the case, it can often impact on the relationship—and sometimes they can think that it is the relationship that is at fault, when in reality it is that their life is out of balance and important needs are not being met.

Some people feel that all their emotional needs must be met by their partner; because of this, they can become over-dependent on their partner.

Dependence makes us unhealthily reliant on one person. If that relationship breaks down or the other person becomes seriously ill or incapacitated, we are on our own. One partner being over-dependent on the other can put both partners under a lot of strain. To get our needs met in balance, we probably need to be inter-dependent.

Independence is where we are self-reliant and stand on our own feet.

Dependence is when we get most or all of our needs met through one other person. This is sometimes called co-dependence when two people are over- reliant on one another.

Inter-dependence is increasingly seen as the healthiest model. Inter-dependence is when we are self-reliant but meets our needs through a range of relationships and activities (such as friends, family, neighbors and colleagues).

Inter-dependence leaves us more resilient in the face of adversity. It gives us multiple sources of the things that we need.

Our Essential Emotional Needs14 is:

Safety—Freedom from experiencing real or imagined danger.

Security—the ability to plan and feel confident about important aspects of our lives, such as our finances, our employment, our living arrangements, and our relationships.

Belonging to a wider community—this may be, for instance, a community of neighbors, friends, a social or sports club, members of a religious or spiritual community, or a political group.

Privacy—Time on our own to reflect on our lives and consolidate new learning, and to deal, without embarrassment, with our bodily functions.

Emotional connection—A sense of being known and understood by at least one other person. Knowing that someone is there for us and that we can be completely ourselves with them.

Control—the ability to make decisions about at least some aspects of our lives.

Giving and receiving attention—Feeling that we are giving & receiving enough attention.

Swapping attention with healthy individuals helps to keep us sane. It allows us to check our own model of reality against other people's models. It stops us from losing our moorings and helps keep us grounded.

However, it is essential that the people we swap attention with regularly are reasonably healthy; otherwise we may just reinforce a view of reality that is distorted.

For example, people who tend to get depressed need to be careful not to spend too much time with others who are depressed because of the danger of themselves taking on an unhealthily pessimistic and negative view of the world.

Meaning and purpose—our need for meaning can be met in many ways by contributing positively to our families, our communities, and the wider world and by living in congruence with our deepest values.

WEEK 6: SPIRITUALITY

Romans

"For to set the mind on the flesh is death, but to set the mind on the Spirit is life and peace."

The beauty of each partnership is that it is unique. Your commitment to your partner does not need to look like anyone else's commitment. What-ever the two of you agree on is fine. You may decide that you want to live together or to live separately. You may decide that you want to be sexual together or not. If you are sexual, you may decide to be exclusive or not. It's all a matter of what you both are comfortable with.

The sacredness of your commitment to your partnership does not lie in its specific content so much as it does in its mutuality and in your willingness to abide by it. Your commitment is your covenant with your partner.

The first rule of agreement-making is: be honest with your partner. Don't pretend to be someone you are not. Don't make an agreement you can't keep just because you are trying to please your partner. Your honesty here will save you a lot of pain down the line.

A commitment does not mean anything if you can't keep it. Your ability to keep the commitment is what makes it a commitment. So never promise what you can't deliver. If your partner expects you to be faithful and you know that you have trouble being faithful to one person, don't promise to be faithful. Say "I'm sorry. I can't promise that."

Then, your partner might say "Then I can't be sexual with you" or s/he might say "Okay, I'll be sexual with you as long as you are faithful to me. If you sleep with someone else, will you agree to tell me immediately?" And this might be a request that you can honor.

Based on this interchange, the nature of the proposed commitment has changed. You aren't saying "I commit to being faithful to you." You are saying "I commit to tell you immediately if I sleep with someone else."

For the sake of balance and fairness in the relationship, the commitments you make should be mutual, not unilateral. It is a spiritual law that you cannot receive what you are unwilling to give. So, don't expect a commitment from your partner that you are unwilling to make yourself. Unilateral commitments lead to some form of abuse or betrayal, not just for one partner, but for both.

When you make a commitment and realize that you cannot keep it, tell your partner right away. Suppose you commit to living with your partner and after a month of doing so, you are really miserable. You don't have the privacy or the quiet time you want. You resent the other person's presence and you find yourself being critical of your partner in ways that surprise you.

Don't be stoical and say "I made this commitment and I'm going to keep it no matter what." Shoving your feelings will only exacerbate your dissatisfaction, and you are likely to become even more passive-aggressive in expressing your discomfort with the situation. Instead, tell your partner that you need to talk. "I know that I made the commitment to live with you," you can say, "but I need to tell you that I've been having a really hard time honoring that commitment. I'm feeling resentful toward you because I'm not getting the space and the quiet time I need. I know that's not your fault, but it doesn't seem to matter. I'm blaming you anyway. I don't want to do that anymore. I think I might need to reconsider this whole thing. It may be that I need to live alone."

Your partner might not be too overjoyed to hear these words coming out of your mouth, but they may help him or her understand what's been going on for you. Chances are that your partner has been sensing your unhappiness and may be feeling responsible for it. When you own your feelings and tell your partner "I know it's not your fault. This is about me. I got in over my head. I underestimated the space I needed," your partner can stop feeling responsible for your pain.

When you ask to re-negotiate your commitment, you are basically acknowledging to your partner that you made a mistake. You are asking for understanding and forgiveness. You are asking for the opportunity to make a choice that honors yourself and the other person equally.

It is a spiritual law that you cannot honor another person by betraying yourself. Self-betrayal ultimately leads to betrayal of your partner, because sooner or later you are going to realize that you made a commitment you cannot keep. Better to face the embarrassment of that mistake than continue to make it. If your partner cannot forgive you, then you can work on forgiving yourself and being more clear in the future about what you need and want.

This is not to say that we should take our commitments lightly. We should always endeavor to keep our promises. To do so, we might sometimes have to override a selfish desire and act with restraint. Or we may need to make the long term well-being of our children or other important people in our life a bigger priority than our short-term comfort.

In the past, people made lifetime commitments before they knew themselves or their partners intimately. Since divorces were rare, those commitments often led to lives of mutual sacrifice and denial. People stayed together even though they were miserable. Obviously, this extreme of staying together at all costs is not desirable.

Today, we face the other extreme. More people are getting divorced than are staying together. People are not willing to compromise even in little ways to keep their relationships together. Many people leave their relationships before they have really given them a chance. Lessons are not being learned. Families are being broken up. People take the easy way out and then have to deal with the guilt they feel about their actions.

Commitments are serious business. Couples should be conservative and make realistic commitments. Marriage is not the only commitment available to people today. After three to

184

five years living together, it might be realistic for a couple to be discussing a lifetime commitment. But a couple that has been dating for a year simply doesn't have enough information or experience to make such a long-term decision.

Nonetheless, it is not uncommon in our society for two nineteen-year-olds to be talking about marriage. That is not only unrealistic, it is asking for trouble. At nineteen, you don't know who you are and what you want. You have to take time to find out. At this stage of life, a commitment of six months or a year is more realistic. If things go well after a year, a longer term commitment can be made.

Even when a couple has been together for six months or a year, they should be conservative in making commitments. For example, it would not be realistic for them to commit to having children right away, since their relationship has not been fully tested. How can they possibly know after six months or a year if their partnership is strong enough to weather the emotional demands of being parents?

If you and your partner make an unrealistic commitment, there is a good chance that one or both of you won't be able to live up to it. It is better to make smaller commitments and fulfill them than it is to make a large commitment and have to re-negotiate it. When you shoot too high in a relationship, it can be painful to pick up the pieces and it may be difficult to reestablish mutual trust. Remember, small successes build mutual confidence and lead naturally to the making of more substantial commitments. So be conservative in the commitment you make to one another. Let it be a commitment that you know that you can keep.

It you commit to living with someone and you aren't able to honor the commitment, you need to look carefully at that fact. Perhaps you did not know yourself or the other person well enough when you made the commitment to live together. A more realistic commitment might have been to see each other every other day and on the weekends while still living separately. That would have given you a sense of what living together might have been like before you attempted to put your lives together.

Commitment is one of the most difficult areas of relationship. Without it, people don't feel safe being together. They don't know where they stand with each other. Mutual commitment helps both people feel safe. But that safety is not real if the commitment isn't realistic.

It is a harsh reality of life that many of our relationship commitments are broken. That's because many of us are over-committing or committing before we are ready. We need to slow things down and take the time to get to know each other before making agreements.

The following is a list of four progressive relationship commitments leading toward a lifetime commitment. The list is not comprehensive, nor is its definitions and timetables rigid. It is meant only as a suggestion or a guide to help you and your partner get clear on the kind of commitment you can make to each other. Please use this list as a springboard for discussing how you and your partner would define your relationship, where you stand on the issue of fidelity, and what timeframe feels comfortable to both of you.

WEEK 7: INTIMACY

Hebrews 13:4

"Let marriage be held in honor among all, and let the marriage bed be undefiled, for God will judge the sexually immoral and adulterous."

- Is it possible to experience ongoing emotional intimacy and sensual passion in a long-term relationship?

- Will we be able to sustain our erotic connection?

- Can we create a fantastic sex life, even if we never had one to begin with?

These questions plague many couples; couples who love one another deeply. They whisper in the background when you yearn to feel intimate connection with your beloved, when you yearn to feel cherished and adored. And the questions simmer to the surface as you want to be supported in becoming the best version of yourself. You also want to be the kind of person who offers this quality of connection to your partner. But you can't figure out how.

Maybe you have read a number of books on how to improve your relationship, or how to improve yourself. Maybe you have done therapy at one point or another, experiencing short-term benefits which didn't last. Maybe you don't really know what you want anymore, because it feels too hard to figure it out. And if you did know, you wouldn't know how to create it anyway. Yet you are absolutely certain that you both want to stay together, so it really is worthwhile to figure out how to enjoy one another more.

These mostly unspoken challenges linger in the air, silently. You only really notice them in the rare moments you are alone, or when you look through old photographs and feel an ache for rekindled connection. Or perhaps you feel jealous when you see a friend from college in a happy flirtatious photo with her husband while on vacation. You want so badly to feel how she feels, to have what she appears to have. Mostly though, you don't let these thoughts derail you because there is so much good in your life. You and your partner are devoted to your family, to the raising of your children, and to providing for all their needs. For the most part, you don't doubt that he's the right partner for you.

Even so, you aren't happy, and you can't figure out what to do about it.

First of all, let me tell you that you are not alone, far from it!

As a society, we are collectively struggling in our attempts to build lasting relationships. The divorce rate is staggeringly high as is the huge percentage of couples who are dissatisfied with the quality of their relationship.

While maintaining a relationship is obviously challenging, this book is not about staying together. It is for you, because you do want to stay together. You and your partner are committed, and the question is not about whether to stay together. It is how!

- How do you co-create a relationship that fulfills your true yearning, one that doesn't just look good on the outside, but truly feeds your soul?

- How do you create a relationship that fuels your purpose, and brings delight and play to every day?

- How do you create a relationship with both planned and spontaneous adventures to places you want to visit?

- How do you create a relationship where you feel the solidity that comes with knowing someone well, plus the delight that comes with discovering new things, having new experiences, and learning more about your partner?

The problem of how is completely understandable. Because as mammals, one of the primary ways we learn is through imitation. But when we look around for great long-term relationships worthy of emulation, we come up very short. And when we don't have strong imprinting, it's hard to know how.

When I first became a relationship coach, early in working with a couple, I used to ask them whom they admired. What were the relationships that inspired them and motivated them – either in their own family, or in their extended network of friends and acquaintances, or in movies, literature, or celebrities? Every time the couple would look at one another, wondering, and come up empty. I never had anyone answer the question with clarity and conviction so eventually I stopped asking. In the process I learned much about the lack of role-model couples along with the huge need for them.

This isn't to say that there aren't people who really admire the love their parents or grandparents share. But that doesn't mean it is the relationship they want to be experiencing. Times change rapidly with the generations and what worked for your grandparents is unlikely to work for you. Consider how gender roles are different, women's relationship to work and purpose has changed, and our expectation of what we will experience in a marriage has evolved. What that means is that we have an overload of examples of long-term committed relationships which are not what we are looking for, and a dearth of those that would be worthwhile aspiring to. In other words, we lack a roadmap, or as I like to say, a blueprint for the kind of relationship we yearn for.

The research is consistent with this dilemma: While the divorce rate is high, the data on those who stay together is equally discouraging. Actually, we don't have very much data because there are few entities that fund such research. When it comes to incidence and patterns of disease, or even education, there are many corporations that see financial benefit in collecting data, but that isn't true when it comes to relationships. One exception to this is Durex, the condom maker. As part of a study, the Durex Company interviewed

29,000 couples and found that 54 percent were dissatisfied with the quality of their relationships. Other research has shown that up to 84 percent of married couples aren't happy with the intimacy they experience.

In working with couples, I have discovered that there are three main kinds of relationships: toxic, termination, and toleration:

A toxic relationship is one in which fear and anger govern most interactions. This can involve violence and abuse of various kinds. A toxic relationship doesn't have a safe enough container to do the work in this book. If you are reading this book and that is your situation, I encourage you to turn to another resource for support and return to this book when your relationship is more stable.

In a termination relationship, one or both people have already given up on the relationship. Maybe you have already filed for divorce, or perhaps you are waiting to do so for one reason or another. There are often significant financial reasons to stay together, or you need psychological stability and are not ready to rock the boat. In fact, one in four couples stay together until all the children are out of the house; they stay together for the sake of the children even though they would otherwise separate. If you are in a termination relationship, there will be valuable material for you in this book which you can use to improve the mood in your home. You will learn how to co-parent and co-create with your spouse in a way that is more satisfying for both of you. However, the promise of this book – to show you the path to create emotional intimacy and passionate, deeply satisfying sex, is for readers who are in relationships where both of you are committed to the relationship and willing to do what it takes to make it fantastic.

If you are, in fact, committed to making the relationship work, you may be in the third kind of relationship, the toleration relationship. The vast majority of couples are in toleration relationships. These are relationships where they have learned to live with things that don't feel great and don't really work for them, but they are overriding their unmet needs and desires in order to save the relationship.

In the toleration relationship, there is no question whether you love each other, because you really do. Furthermore, there are countless things you love about the life you have built together. You can depend on one another to show up for your children, to be punctual to important events, to do your best to provide for your family, and to be there for each other most of the time. But, despite all of this felt love and evidence of commitment, your life together feels relatively stable, mundane, and unfulfilling. It might be painful to admit, because in a toleration relationship the hurt is often buried deep below the surface. In fact, it's important to you that your relationship looks good on the outside; you don't want to trouble your kids and you certainly don't want others to think there is anything wrong. You may think to yourself that so many other couples deal with much bigger problems, so why focus on what isn't working.

WEEK 8: LEARN TO COMMUNICATE ALWAYS

Ephesians 4:29

"Let no corrupting talk come out of your mouths, but only such as is good for building up, as fits the occasion, that it may give grace to those who hear."

192

Why do you interact with your husband? This can be a challenging task especially if your partner doesn't want to speak to you. But look no further, even if you don't know where to start, the steps below will help you connect with your spouse. It will also help you boost communication when things aren't going well in your marriage. And it begins with you putting the seven basic steps that we share below into practice. We have made much use of these basic measures to strengthen communication in our marriage and we have had great successes. Personally, we agree that these communication techniques can allow you to start interacting with your spouse better today.

And if your partner doesn't want to practice them with you, you should practice them every day and it will strengthen your marriage.

1. May I please get your attention? It is here that you learn active listening. Make sure both you and your partner listen and pay attention to each other while you're having a discussion. When your partner doesn't listen, or pay attention, you won't hear all of your "verbs." If your partner asks you something, sit and listen. We will be able to meet you. Really listen, not just listen. What you need to do is listen closely to what your partner is saying to you. Don't disturb and put away distractions as they talk. Due to how "busy" we are all, it is very easy to distract ourselves these days. Distractions make communication very difficult, particularly when it comes to listening, paying full attention and engaging in the conversation. What you interact affects the world that you are in. A great way to start is by telling your partner when it would be a good time to have their focus undivided. Make sure it's not because your partner is too fatigued, stressed or overloaded emotionally.

2. No shouting. Don't scream at your spouse when you're trying to get a message across or talk to each other. It just isn't setting the tone for effective communication. Will you want to yell at your spouse? Ironically, we are shouting to be heard so it just causes the partner to scream back or shut down entirely. Speak to them in a calm and polite way, who you want to be referred to. If you feel too upset, or frustrated, take a break and revisit when both of you are calm. Be polite of your speech and be caring.

3. A mile in your wife's heels. If you have a debate, disagreement or just speak, try to look at the topic from the point of view of your partner. Seek to understand where the partner comes from and continue listening empathetically. It will help you to understand what your partner is trying to tell you. How does your partner understand best what you're trying to tell them? Mind that they do think differently from you.

4. Strengthen awareness. Just explain! Tell your partner if they understand what you're trying to talk to them about. When they understand you completely let them explain it to you. What are the words which they use? How does the term signify? This works to make you understand where they are about what you are trying to communicate. Don't say that when you think something is wrong, everything is ok. Mean what you tell your husband. When you're in a noisy environment it's hard to hear, let alone listen and understand what the other person says. Make sure that the atmosphere in which you are is sufficient enough to clearly hear each other, to be able to understand and to communicate well. Do not be afraid to ask when you're not hearing anything. Rather than later it is better to ask now.

4. Changing your game and hitting home run. When the partner doesn't understand what you have written, try to convey it to them using different methods. Seek various verbal examples, analogies or even pictures depending on what you are trying to convey. You may also use diagram drawing, on paper writing, etc. When you don't understand something, or have not heard your spouse say it, don't be shy. Tell them to repeat what they've been saying and describe it in a way that you understand.

6. Take a rest. If you don't make progress in expressing a thought, concept, question or start feeling irritated, take a break. Review later after each of you has had time to think about the problem. That's so necessary, and very helpful. Perhaps it's just time to re-evaluate.

7. Repeat and rinse. Any time you connect with your partner, apply the above techniques. Know, the trick is being open-minded, listening carefully and having patience!

The pair's desire and willingness are necessary to enhance communication in every marriage. And you need to recognize that you and your partner must make a deliberate effort to connect effectively in your marriage.

Additionally, by knowing how to better communicate with your spouse, you can avoid most of the communication issues, and small (even some big) arguments in your marriage.

Marriage is Impossible without Trust

Trust is a critical part of communication. A stable marriage partnership can't exist without confidence. Communication with each other, without confidence, will not be as successful. If you don't like them should you believe what your spouse says?

The problems of confidence in marriage can be induced by physical affairs, deception, emotional affairs, and contact with an ex, pornography, etc. The lack of confidence creates uncertainty, in general. Building full trust in your marriage should also be a priority, because it contributes to a deeper level of healthy contact. Being able to trust your husband or wife gives you the confidence and freedom to express yourself entirely. Trust gives you the freedom to feel comfortable enough to share with your partner any part of yourself, without fear of rejection or guilt. Likewise, your partner needs to be able to trust that the deep intimate issues you are thinking about and communicating with each other stay between you two.

"Intimacy comes from deep-seated" knowing "the other person. When there are obstacles to authenticity, information is omitted and the false takes over. "(Boundaries in Marriage.) In order for both of you to feel secure enough to bare one another's hearts, to be vulnerable emotionally with your partner, and to connect better, you must develop mutual trust. One of the best things marriage can bring is genuinely understanding someone, making them know you, being truly loved and appreciated for who you are. Getting profoundly attached to another human getting, gives us meaning in life. They would do anything for the bond as people, which is why others are turning to addictive behaviors.

"We have a strong desire for bonding and forming relations. It's our way of getting our happiness. When we can't connect with each other, we'll connect with everything that we can find. "This doesn't happen overnight to create trust in marriage. It just needs time and purpose. It will take some extra work if either you or your partner from previous relationships has had issues of confidence.

Start by making sure your partner is completely truthful. Have you ever told your spouse anything about your plans for the past, the present or even the future? To make full faith a fact in your marriage, make sure that you are trustworthy. Tell your spouse when you're overspending on a budget item. If you feel like you've started having thoughts about someone other than your spouse, or feel like you might have done something that your spouse wouldn't want to do if roles were reversed, just have a chat to resolve it.

If you're upset by something, when you haven't done anything that you said you'd, and the list continues. Be an open spousal journal. Share your thoughts, in particular the daily stresses and challenges you go through. Don't be afraid to ask questions about them. It won't be simple all the time, but the more trust you develop, the more open and connected you is to your spouse. Never put your spouse in danger! You will feel upset when you do so, and not comfortable around you. That would mean they aren't as available with you. Do your utmost never to say something that hurt your partner deliberately for the sake of injury.

You can't be afraid to rock the boat and hide your thoughts, or things. This means you're not only lying to your partner but you are lying to yourself. Stuffing stuff inside of you and not being able to express your feelings properly in a safe way can be harmful to your wellbeing, as well as to your relationship. You're making it build up by not getting it out in the open, which can become anger against your partner. If you allow all these little items to pile up, anything insignificant will finally explode. These turn into rage and frustration when you bottle up your emotions. When you can't be frank and emotionally transparent to your partner or you, something deeper is happening that hinders truthful contact.

197

Could a tiny white lie really do a lot of harm to a marriage? Through omission, what about lying? No hurt, right no foul? Incorrect. The response to that is clear. Lies, or not saying the truth to your partner so what they don't know does not harm them, erodes the basic cornerstone of your marriage, which is trust. This makes you feel guilty, which makes it difficult on a deeper level to be genuinely intimate.

"The disappointment destroys a friendship. The act of lying is much more destructive than the things that are being lied about; because lying destroys each other's awareness and the connection itself ... Deception is the one thing that cannot be worked around because it denies the issue. "-Dr. Cloud, Henry.

You will think this is an enormous amount of information to share, what if you forget something? They are all examples which will help you understand the small areas better. You can start by ensuring your spouse is trustworthy. If your partner is asking you something, they need to know it will remain between you two. Do not run to your best friend or family member, if you have an argument. Eight out of ten occasions that is due to a miscommunication. When you run to a member of your family, parents, or relative, they'll see your spouse in a different light, which you can't take back so quickly. They don't think you do love your mom.

WEEK 9: RESOLVE CONFLICTS

Matthew 7:1-11:30

"Judge not, that you be not judged. For with the judgment you pronounce you will be judged, and with the measure you use it will be measured to you. Why do you see the speck that is in your brother's eye, but do not notice the log that is in

198

your own eye? Or how can you say to your brother, 'Let me take the speck out of your eye,' when there is the log in your own eye? You hypocrite, first take the log out of your own eye, and then you will see clearly to take the speck out of your brother's eye. ..."

Conflicts are bound to happen in a relationship one time or the other. How you deal with them will determine whether yours will stand the test of time or not. When you fight with your spouse, how can you tell if you will be able to address the issues at hand in an amicable manner?

Well, the truth is that a strong relationship will not seek to reduce conflict. This is mainly because there will always be conflict in any relationship, and there is nothing you can do to prevent that from ever happening. When you choose a partner, the fact is that you chose a certain set of problems. They come as a package!

If you are looking for a partner that you will never have to fight with, get mad at, or even complain about, then you will never find one, at least not in this world. While it is often difficult to believe, fighting in a relationship is good. According to research, it is evident that a couple that does not fight at least three years into the relationship is indicative of an unhealthy marriage.

A healthy relationship is one that is stable but also has a healthy conflict. Arguing with your spouse is not a sign that you are destined for doom. Understand that this is all healthy and normal. The trick is for you to focus on addressing the problem instead of attacking each other. Once you resolve the issue, you choose to forget each other for the parts you contributed and move on.

According to a marriage therapist, Jeanette Raymond, the true measure of a strong relationship is how fast you resolve issues and reunite. If you are looking to cultivate a strong, happy, and long-lasting marriage, then you have to be willing always to take the initiative to have each other's back and embrace one another even when you have a difference of opinion or disagreements.

My wife and I have made it a rule that even when we disagree; we have to resolve our issues before going to bed. No one signed up to spend their night on the couch. We address our issues and go to bed, talking to each other.

But what do you do if there are poor conflicts in your relationship?

The truth is this is a sign that your relationship is unhealthy. That said you must make a choice not to stay angry with your spouse after fighting. One mistake I have seen couples make is hold a grudge even long after the disagreements has been infused. Others choose to sweep issues under the carpet instead of addressing them head-on. What is even worse is that other couples freeze their emotions and completely shut down as though the rest of the world does not exist.

You must work with your spouse to rebuild the emotional connection that you once had together. Make it a commitment to restore security into your relationship. You can do this by first ensuring that you override your hurt feelings. Choose to be happy rather than being right. When you hold a grudge against your partner, you are simply choosing to breed resentment that will eventually destroy your marriage.

Understand that it is not about what you are fighting about; it is how you choose to fight!

WEEK 10: THE SMALL STUFF

Romans 8:28

"And we know that for those who love God all things work together for good, for those who are called according to his purpose."

Amazingly, more marriages break up over the little stuff than over the big stuff. It is easier, sometimes, to forgive someone for having spent the rent (although that isn't a good move, and can lead to some pretty scary results) than it is for having perpetually bad breath or always having sharp toenails that cause pain during intimate moments. When it comes to the small stuff, there are three good solutions:

•   Apologize, and then try not to repeat the offense. In spite of the 1970s catch phrase from the movie, Love Story, those two little words, "I'm sorry," when said sincerely can heal a whole heap of hurt.

•   Remember to say "Thank you." Don't save up for those big occasions like anniversaries and birthdays, say it often. Say it with flowers, with treats, with hugs and kisses. And remember actually to say the words – don't count on your actions to do it for you. Say it with your behavior, too. Show your appreciation for paid bills, well cooked meals, a clean house or mown lawn. You and your dearest might be able to afford a trip to Las Vegas or Disney Land once in a while, but saying "Thank you" doesn't destroy the budget or run the risk of being the wrong brand or color. Look for good things, find reasons to say it and mean it.

- Say I love you. Like "Thank you," "I love you," needs to be said in words. It also needs to be said in deeds. It is never hard to find unlovable things in human beings, and focusing in on those will lead to hard and angry words. Look for the things you love, like the wayward curl that will never behave, no matter how much hair goop gets layered over it, or the laugh crinkles at the corners of the eyes. See if you can wake up those laugh crinkles.

These three things won't necessarily patch a marriage that has fallen on hard times, but they can go a long way toward fixing a great many things. They go together very nicely with things like honesty, understanding and communication. There is one small catch, however: they work best when you truly mean them and when you try your hardest not to do things that require you to say you are sorry, when you look for all the things your beloved does for which you can say thank you, and – above all – when you can say "I love you," and truly mean it.

With these three phrases, you can remedy the fusses that come from those unthinking incidents, such as squeezing the toothpaste tube in the middle or finding toenail trimmings on the clean sheets, or the trail of ants to your spouse's side of the bed – thanks to his or her habit of eating in bed. Or even situations that arise from events such as a hearty fart in the middle of a dinner party. Which brings up another useful phrase, "Excuse me?" It is such a simple phrase, "excuse me" and it can be quietly murmured. It is preferable to looking around and saying loudly, "I didn't do it." Or, alternatively, saying, "Who did that? Did you do it?" while your spouse is wishing that the floor would open up and swallow her or him.

Practice simple courtesy at home in ways that are considerate and kind. A few folks might consider such things as a sign of weakness; rather, it is a sign of inner strength that can acknowledge wrongs and perhaps even a laugh with your dearest at your own failings. It is the simple glue that will get you past mistakenly discussing politics or religion with your in-laws or failing to praise an old family recipe.

2 Peter 3:18

"But grow in the grace and knowledge of our Lord and Savior Jesus Christ. To him be the glory both now and to the day of eternity. Amen."

The partner you choose to marry was never perfect, so they may, at times, be a cause of disappointment and discouragement. You will feel down; things will be said that may cause hurt. They are sometimes self-centered, impatient and insensitive, so you see the good, the bad and the ugly protruding daily as you live and grow together. How do you respond to your spouse's mistakes? Do you complain incessantly and criticize her/him with your family? Do you allow the children to hear your rebuke and see your disappointment? Do you belittle your spouse by making sarcastic comments to friends, causing your together forever partner to be looked down upon?

There is no perfect marriage because there is no perfect spouse. It is not about being perfect; it is about perfecting until Jesus comes. Today, consider how you both are falling into sin. Why not take a moment to share what you see. Speak the truth in love, offer forgiveness and understanding and continue to pray one for another. Just do this, since you are not innocent yourself and you both need God's amazing grace.

Matthew 6:14-15

"For if you forgive others their trespasses, your heavenly Father will also forgive you, but if you do not forgive others their trespasses, neither will your Father forgive your trespasses."

Be ready to forgive just as easily as you'd like to be forgiven when on the wrong. Accept apologies gracefully without any conditions. Don't count how many times you've forgiven your spouse, once you resolve a conflict you move on. Give them the benefit of the doubt. Probably they were disappointed or angry when they did what they did, or probably you may have driven them over the edge. Probably they never took the time to figure out the impact of their actions.

Conflicts are a common occurrence in any marriage. Different backgrounds and personalities coming together will inevitably lead to some disagreements here and there. Expectations and unfamiliar habits, life's challenges and different outlook of life will fuel these conflicts. A healthy relationship must have disagreements. What couples must learn to do is to resolve these conflicts amicably. They should learn to disagree peacefully. You surely won't have to agree with everything, but you have to find a way round your disagreements. Unresolved conflicts can lead to a rise in tensions, anger and frustrations in the marriage which will be disastrous in the long term.

The first step in understanding your partner and your differences is knowing and adjusting to each other's personalities. Often in marriages, you marry someone who is opposite of you so that you find slow paced people marrying someone who goes through life at great speeds. Task-oriented people will be attracted to a people-oriented person. An outgoing personality might be attracted to a more reserved person. Make a point of understanding your spouse and their kind of personality. When you understand them, you appreciate their opinions and it's easier to make compromises.

Resolving conflicts requires us to confront each other lovingly. Your spouse is or should eventually be your best friend. A good friend isn't supposed just to keep quiet when they realize that their friend is doing something not right. You need to go to them with love and show them where they have gone wrong. Check your words and emotions lest they are mistaken to mean you are pursuing a fight. The purpose of the confrontation should be to draw you closer together in love. It shows you care so much about your spouse and your marriage that you want to make things right. Choose an appropriate time and setting to do this. Listen to their side of things and don't mix up issues. Focus on the problem not necessarily the person and do not use accusatory words such as "you are." don't look to win the argument at all. In a marriage, there is no winning and losing as this can make you deviate from the facts of the matter. You might focus so much on winning and indeed win the argument but lose your spouse.

Despite your differences with your spouse, do not apply the cold shoulder treatment. This is far much worse than a fight. If you feel you don't want to discuss anything with them at the moment, let them know and you can set aside another time to talk about it.

WEEK 13: ALWAYS HELP EACH OTHER IN DIFFICULTIES

Psalm 34:17

"When the righteous cry for help, the Lord hears and delivers them out of all their troubles."

Generosity is one of the most important marital values. If you want to be a better partner to your spouse, you have to be more of a giver than a receiver.

Here are some of the ways that you can show generosity and care with your partner:

1. Be generous with your time.

Nowadays, time is the most important, but limited resource. If you have been spending too much time building your career, now is the time to take a step back and spend more time with your spouse. Here are some ways that you can do to spend quality time with your partner:

- Reminisce and recreate your first date together. If your marriage is falling apart, it would help if you recreate your very first date together. Did you have a fancy dinner at a high-end restaurant? Did you watch the Knicks game? Did you watch a movie or did you have a casual lunch at Kentucky Fried Chicken? Recreating your first date is a type of emotional time travel that will not only rekindle the lost spark in the relationship. It will also allow you to spend more time with your partner.

- Take a vacation together. You and your spouse may be dealing with a lot of money problems, bills or problems with the kids. Take a step back and go on a vacation with your spouse.

- Have a movie night together. Just sit down in your living room or your bedroom and watch a good movie. You can also watch your favorite TV series together.

2. Express gratitude and appreciation. Be generous with praise.

Expressing gratitude and appreciation is the best way that you can be emotionally generous to your partner or spouse. Thank your spouse for all the good things that he has done for you. Also, thank your partner for being there for you. Thank your partner for being kind, for giving you gifts, and for doing errands for you.

Disarm your spouse by giving genuine and sincere compliments. You would be surprised to learn that praise and compliment can actually save a marriage.

3. Express love.

When you are expressing love for your partner, you are being emotionally generous. Say "I love you" as often as you can. Hold your spouse's hand as you walk. Give him or her a kiss as you leave for work. Tell your spouse how much he or she means to you. Let your partner know that he or she is valuable to you.

4. Give your spouse a gift even on ordinary days.

It is expected of you to give your spouse a gift during special occasions. However, it is good to give your spouse a gift every now and then for no reason. This will make your spouse feel special.

If you are a guy, then give your wife flowers every month. If you are a woman, then surprise your husband with a new tie, an expensive wine, or a new watch.

Remember that it is always better to give than to receive. Many studies show that recipients are often satisfied with the relationship. However, the givers are often more satisfied and happier with the marriage. According to psychologists, it is better to give than receive in marriage.

Be selfless. Think of your partner's welfare and happiness. Give your spouse all the things, emotional support and love that you can give.

WEEK 14: ALWAYS KEEP THE RELATIONSHIP LIVELY

Hebrews 13:4

"Let marriage be held in honor among all, and let the marriage bed be undefiled, for God will judge the sexually immoral and adulterous."

A commitment of unconditional love is the widely accepted description and definition of marriage. This vivid portrayal also captures the underlying driving force of a happy and long-lasting marriage – romance.

Romance is the outward portrayal, expression, and demonstration of love. Therefore, the intensity, frequency, and sustenance are a surefire thermometer to establish the position and strength of your relationship. Romance is also a sure indication of the contentment of partners within a relationship.

In marriage, the traditional expectations of a family driven by culture and conventions are involved in gauging and influencing the relationship. However, romance still retains its crucial role as the glue that nourishes relationships and keeps them going even during rocky times.

In building and sustaining a marriage, there is a need to cultivate oneness and bolster intimacy. You and your partner have to be committed to meet each other's emotional and physical needs. Marriage faces significant dynamism and changes. Marriage partners might fail to hold high levels of commitment at all times. As a result, there is a need for a problem-solving approach. When the relationship hits trouble, there is a need for a way to find a solution. In the second or third year of marriage, something typically happens in most marriages. The romantic heat that warmed the relationship before marriage dies down somewhat. The decline of romance leads to a plummeting of the ability of these partners to meet each other's physical and emotional needs. This increases the chances of conflict and the likelihood of divorce or separation. The question here is – how do you guard against the dying passion and fires of romance?

Is there is something about marriages that seems to kill romantic motivation and creativity? At some point in their marriages, couples realize that they no longer take each other to feel the passion, desire, and romance that they once did.

There are ways you can re-introduce, utilize, and sustain romance within a married setting. Here are some of the ways to keep the excitement, passion, and heat of love alive within your marriage. This way, it will nourish your relationship with the emotional and physical satisfaction required to you and your spouse happy.

Romance ought to be part of your daily diet

The concept of love, especially in marriage, refers to the unconditional love and robust commitment of the partners to their partners. Romance is essential in a marriage because it is the daily manifestation of this love towards your partner. Romance is the fuel that keeps the marriage engine running. If it dies down, then everything else comes tumbling down.

Keeping romance in your daily diet means deliberately resolving to do romantic things or actions for your partner. Complement her good looks. For example, for the husband, notice how good she looks, her good mood, how good she smells, and how she makes you feel. Tell her how much you love and desire her body, and how crazy she makes you feel.

Visualizing her and letting her know about how you feel allows her to feel appreciated. It also lets her in on your thoughts, affection, love, appreciation, and attachment to her. It helps keep the romance levels high and maintain the connection you have into the marriage period.

Partners are typically good friends. However, there is a part of your relationship that goes beyond friendship. You share a marriage bed, dreams, and thoughts that are shared with no one else in the world. Therefore, making romance part of your daily interactions helps keep it alive.

This approach also develops it into a good habit to appreciate your partner every day with the same vigor and passion you did before you got married. Such a decision helps marriage through more difficult, challenging, and disruptive circumstances. For example, after the birth of your first child, the relationship and romance might be eclipsed by the attention given to the child and the accompanying chores.

WEEK 15: SMILE AND PLAY TOGETHER

Proverbs 15:13-14

"A glad heart makes a cheerful face, but by sorrow of heart the spirit is crushed. The heart of him who has understanding seeks knowledge, but the mouths of fools feed on folly."

A happy relationship is a stable relationship. A good sense of humor is always a big plus in every relationship. Laughter can be used to heal rifts in a relationship. People would generally hang around someone who makes them laugh; this is why comedians make so much money.

Play Games Together

Games are generally seen as a male vocation, but that doesn't mean that there aren't female gamers out there. A study done in the Queensland University of Technology concluded that multiplayer video games help in building solid emotional relationships between gamers. Gaming doesn't only apply to video games; couples can enjoy card or board games. Playing games with your partner helps to improve romantic connection while reducing stress at the same time. Friendly competition is advised, cutthroat competitions only leave both sides feeling bad at the end of the game.

Spice Things Up

It is no secret that couples fall into some grey area after a while together. They end up doing the same thing, over and over again. At first, this might seem reasonable and unharmful, but in the long run, this would lead to boredom in the relationship. A couple should endeavor not to fall into this trap of comfort, by spicing things up once in a while. This can be achieved by merely breaking from the usual routine, once in a while, going on vacations, or more open-mindedness in the bedroom. There are a million and one things a couple can do to ensure that their relationship doesn't get boring. As long as it is safe and exciting, it should be done.

1 Thessalonians

"Give thanks in all circumstances; for this is the will of God in Christ Jesus for you."

Simple acts of gratitude go a long way in showing your partner appreciation. This includes, but isn't restricted to gifts. Simple "thank you" can be enough. Gratitude isn't one-sided, so you shouldn't wait on your partner to give you gifts or be kind to you. A couple that wants to stay together must learn to appreciate each other. If you don't appreciate your partner, someone else will.

Taking care to follow these suggestions, would surely make your relationship as happy as those you see on the big screen and social media, but probably not as popular.

People tend to feel unsatisfied and insecure in relationships when they don't feel appreciated by their partners. When you don't pay attention to your partner, you open the way up for feelings of resentment to grow in the relationship. Every effort put into the relationship should be appreciated. Gratitude on the little things is the most important.

WEEK 17: GIVE AND RECEIVE LOVE

John 3:16

"For God so loved the world, that he gave his only Son, that whoever believes in him should not perish but have eternal life."

Our God is an amazing God. A master planner who thinks through everything. Even though marriage is an earthly thing that ends after we die, God has found very impressive ways of making marriage work especially as a tool of teaching.

Marriage is supposed to teach us how to love as unconditionally as God does. That is why God holds it so highly. Of course, unconditional love is not something that you can develop in one day.

You need to start somewhere and constantly grow in love as you grow spiritually. The two need to grow in tandem as opposed to one leaving the other behind. That is the only way you can achieve love just as God has envisioned it in the bible.

Even though I have loved with my whole heart, expand my boundaries that I may love more with each passing day. That I may be closer to you and love people and my partner the same way that you have loved me.

WEEK 18: FINANCIAL PLANNING AND DECISION-MAKING: WHAT ARE YOUR HABITS?

James 1:5

"If any of you lacks wisdom, let him ask God, who gives generously to all without reproach, and it will be given him."

There is so much potential conflict when it comes to money! The best way to prevent it is to plan ahead. Let's talk about spending money, drafting a budget, and making financial decisions together.

Spending

How each partner spends money—and on what—is such a common area of dissent. It seems as though there's always a spender and a saver in every relationship. There are the impulse spenders, the planful spenders, the never-spenders, the only-the-necessities spenders, and the champagne-taste folks who always want the best of the best. Chances are your spending habits are contextual based on your family of origin and your money story. Are you someone who thinks money gained should be spent and enjoyed? Or are you someone who feels money should be saved for the worst-case scenario? It's crucial that we talk with our partner about how our spending habits differ and how we can meet in the middle.

Budgeting

Making a budget is an easy way to prevent financial conflict and crisis. As with other topics in this book, managing money isn't something we learned in school. (Unless you studied to be an accountant, in which case I guess you can skip this activity.)

So, let's make a budget. You and your partner are going to sit down for a financial business meeting. (Perhaps you've made a budget before. It's okay: Budgets need to be updated at least once a year, if not more.) Take all your knowledge about money stories, areas of conflict when it comes to finances, and what we know about the weirdness of talking about money and lay it all out on the table. Look at your debt together and make sure your contributions to the family (financial or otherwise) feel fair and equitable.

When you make a budget, you want to look at all of your incoming resources and all of the outgoing bills and expenses for a month. Use a spreadsheet to track everything. There will be monthly fixed spending, like a car insurance payment, health care premium, or rent, which stays the same every month. Then there will be spending that's a little more unpredictable, like going out to eat, shopping, or even putting gas in the car. Categorize your spending into needs and wants.

Making a budget is an easy way to prevent financial conflict and crisis.

How's that budget looking? Are you spending more than you're making? If so, is there any discretionary spending that you can get rid of? Maybe you can drop a subscription service or split one with a friend? Is there enough money coming in that you're able to save for your financial goals, too? Do you need to get a side hustle so you and your partner can go on vacation this year? Do your and your partner's contributions feel equal?

Making Money Decisions

I breezed over decisions related to money. I felt we should lay a strong foundation before talking about this subject. What constitutes a small decision financially? What is a big decision? How do you and your partner prioritize spending? How do you and your partner make a final decision about a big-ticket item? Look at the facts, consider the feelings, share your opinions, and find a resolution that suits everyone.

WEEK 19: LISTEN TO ONE ANOTHER

Proverbs 19:20

"Listen to advice and accept instruction, that you may gain wisdom in the future."

As you look toward your wedding day and a lifetime of marriage, one ingredient will need constant attention for your relationship to flourish. I think you already know what it is—communication. You may think you are communicating now. To a certain degree you are communicating; but the two of you haven't yet learned to really speak one another's language. In some ways, each of you is still somewhat of a foreigner to each other. Learn to use your partner's style of thinking and speaking when the two of you interact together. This will help you to understand and to draw closer to each other.

Remember that communication is not only talking, but also silence, a quiet look, a gentle touch.

Discover the best time of the day for each of you to communicate and give each other the gift of your individual attention. Set aside a bit of time each day to sit together, hold hands and share your hearts and your deepest feelings. Make the first four minutes you see one another at the end of the day's work a time of positive interaction through touch and talking.

Do more than talk; listen as well. Listen with your mind, heart, ears and eyes. Remember that nonverbal language can say more than words can. Listening styles also differ, especially between men and women.

True listening requires total attention, no distractions, and not letting your mind formulate what you will say as soon as your partner stops talking. One of the greatest gifts you can give is to listen. Too many discussions become dialogues of the deaf. "Let every man be quick to hear [a ready listener]" (Jas. 1:19, Amp.). Ask your partner when the best time of the day to talk to each other is.

"So please, just listen a few minutes for your turn and I promise I'll listen to you."

Above all, remember who it is who never tires of listening to you.

WEEK 20: THE SPICE OF APPRECIATION

Ruth 2:12

"The Lord repay you for what you have done, and a full reward be given you by the Lord, the God of Israel, under whose wings you have come to take refuge!"

From a young age, you're taught to say thank you and even your parents try their best to appreciate you for every little thing that you do. Even as a toddler, one of the best tools of motivation is appreciation.

The same should be adopted in marriage. Appreciation shows recognition of the good deeds of your partner. When thanking God for blessing you with a great wife or husband, you should not forget to thank your partner as well.

It might not sound as much but, saying "thank you" occasionally among other magic words like "sorry" can go a long way in making your marriage better and stronger. They are simple words that carry a lot of weight and can lead to great positive changes in the atmosphere and effort that your partner places in serving you.

Even as you bear your own little children, some of the most important lessons that you should teach them at a tender age are the art of appreciation for when you teach them when they are young; they never deviate from them even when they grow up.

It is always a great idea to say thank you whenever something good is done to you. It does not matter whether you have received a bouquet of flowers or breakfast a thank you goes a long way.

WEEK 21: STEER CLEAR OF THE DESIRES OF THE BODY

Psalm 37:4-5

"Delight yourself in the Lord, and he will give you the desires of your heart. Commit your way to the Lord; trust in him, and he will act."

Your only hindrance and perhaps the cradle of sin is your flesh. A human being is comprised of the soul and the flesh. In most cases, as much as we know what is right, the demands of the flesh can be overwhelming which might cause us to sin.

A good Christian is one that not only understands the bible but also one that has mastered the art of self-control and is able to fore go the demands of the flesh.

A great example of how the flesh falters is at the Garden of Gethsemane. While Jesus was praying, his disciples were sleeping. They might have wanted to pray but the demand by the flesh to sleep instead was too much.

It is a tall order for any Christian to tame their worldly desires. However, in due course, it is possible. Spiritual fetes like fasting are quickly dampened by a demanding body. You have to be vigilant and diligent in feeding your spirit more than your flesh if you're going to stay true to the narrow path.

WEEK 22: RECONCILIATION OVER RETALIATION

Matthew 18:15-17

"If your brother sins against you, go and tell him his fault, between you and him alone. If he listens to you, you have gained your brother. But if he does not listen, take one or two others along with you, that every charge may be established by the evidence of two or three witnesses. If he refuses to listen to them, tell it to the church. And if he refuses to listen even to the church, let him be to you as a Gentile and a tax collector."

Whenever two people commit to a lifetime together, they'll inevitably argue and experience hurts. That's why it's extremely important to work together toward full reconciliation each time. You have a lifetime to get hurt, and the same lifetime to live with resentment if it's not dealt with.

The Bible's model of reconciliation is designed for resolution of conflict and restoration of relationships. You deal with the conflict to resolve the underlying issue, all with the end goal of restoring the relationship. It's not always easy, but it's always right.

God doesn't set this standard for us lightly, and it's the primary reason Jesus humbled himself to death on the cross. Remember the grace you're given in Christ to be called "God's chosen ones, holy and beloved". He gave his life so you could be reconciled to him. Can you give grace too?

When you function out of fear and pride (sin) you tend to seek retaliation in order to feel better. But when you operate knowing the price Christ paid on your behalf, you're filled with gratitude, grace, the capacity to forgive, and a genuine desire for reconciliation.

WEEK 23: PROTECT THE SANCTITY OF MARRIAGE

Exodus 21:22-25

"When men strive together and hit a pregnant woman, so that her children come out, but there is no harm, the one who hit her shall surely be fined, as the woman's husband shall impose on him, and he shall pay as the judges determine. But if there is harm, then you shall pay life for life, eye for eye, tooth for tooth, hand for hand, foot for foot, burn for burn, wound for wound, stripe for stripe."

When you join together with your spouse, there are going to be a lot of outside forces that can influence your marriage throughout the years. While marriage is designed by God, Satan doesn't like to see the good that comes from it, and often he will send out a lot of roadblocks that make it really hard to stay together in some cases.

When you and your spouse marry, you have to be ready to protect the sanctity of your marriage. Outside of your relationship with God, your marriage should be the most important relationship in your life. But many things can get in the way of it. We assume that these things are more important, and it isn't long before we are missing out on what really matters, pushing our spouse aside, and wondering where our marriage has gone over the years.

It is so important for you to work on protecting the sanctity of your marriage, and to protect it from any of the outside influences that try to convince you that they are more important than this time as a couple. Some of the things that you should be wary of in your relationship include:

Keep away those workaholic tendencies

If you are like many other Americans, you or your spouse's job will be one of the biggest things that will intrude on your relationship. In fact, at least 70 percent of American workers feel that their work is the biggest form of stress that they feel, and about one-third of them report that they feel they are overworked, according to the American Psychological Association.

The office addicted wife and the workaholic husband can sometimes sound like big stereotypes that we laugh at in our favorite shows, but they are really going to represent real mental states that spouses can go through, and which can really cause some negative effects to your marriage.

Simply telling your spouse, or telling you, to work less isn't going to suffice and it won't solve the problem. This is because there are usually some underlying issues that lead to this workaholic. For example, there could be a problem with the attachment where the spouse starts to feel a level of disconnect from their partner and will use their work as a way to escape. Or there could be a problem where the spouse needs approval from others, and this is something that they are going to feel when they are at the office, rather than at home.

If either of you notice that you spend a lot of time at work and it is hard to give that up, even if you know that it is so important to your relationship, it may be time to talk with a therapist. This will help you to know more about your underlying issues that cause all of that overworking and can help you to get the workaholic tendencies to go away.

Avoid any temptations

Infidelity can ruin a lot of relationships, but this doesn't mean that this is the way that it needs to be. The old mantra of "see no evil, hear no evil, speak no evil" can apply well here. In your relationship, there are going to be times when you will run into someone, who isn't your spouse, who you find attractive. But this doesn't mean that you are allowed just to jump in and cheat on your spouse.

All of us may run across someone who we find attractive over the years, even though they aren't our spouse. If you do come across someone like this, and you are worried at all that there is a risk of it getting too much for you to handle while staying faithful to your spouse, then it is best to avoid that path altogether so that you can avoid the temptation.

You have to be careful with technology and the internet as well. There are many times when you can get onto the wrong sites, social media, chat rooms, or more. You can easily meet with strangers, and there are times when you may find them attractive as well. It doesn't take long until boredom online can lead to a relationship that can ruin your relationship, or even pornography with one of the spouses. It is best to find ways to avoid these temptations as much as possible, so they don't come in and cause more issues to the sanctity of your marriage.

Deuteronomy 31:6

"Be strong and courageous. Do not fear or be in dread of them, for it is the Lord your God who goes with you. He will not leave you or forsake you."

Men, like women, are created to need love differently and for good reasons. Compliments, as shown in Song of Solomon, opens up a woman to be more receptive to her husband's initiations and expectations of sexual love. Men, on the other hand, respond more readily to affirmation of his maleness and manhood. It may appear to be the same, but a careful observation will yield the truth of the matter. Men need affirmation; affirmation of his worthiness; affirmation of his strength; affirmation of his physique; affirmation of his ability to provide and protect his home and family. All of this speaks to his maleness and his image of self. Ladies, men do have a need to be needed, and your affirmation strengthens him in this regard.

The Shulamite woman ensured that her man knew he was thought about and sought after. She ensured that he knew he was missed. His importance was affirmed as she kept searching for her beloved along the streets. Dangers of the night did not prohibit her search and when she found him, his worth was made known. She affirmed his strength and spoke adoringly to her need to be with him uninterrupted.

How can you affirm your husband this week? What project is he working on that you can show support for, even without fully understanding it? What visions and dreams can you speak into affirmatively? How can you encourage your man to his next level with your affirmation?

Your man needs your endorsement; he needs your need of him. He wants to be loved for what he does and not always for what you think he should be doing. Affirm him; praise him for all his good work, just as you do your Lord Jesus.

WEEK 25: LEARNING EACH OTHER'S LANGUAGE

Colossians 3:13

"Bearing with one another and, if one has a complaint against another, forgiving each other; as the Lord has forgiven you, so you also must forgive."

You may be familiar with The Five Love Languages by Gary Chapman, which lays out five ways people are naturally inclined to give and receive love: words of affirmation, quality time, receiving gifts, acts of service, and physical touch. When I first read the book and took the accompanying personality test, I discovered that my love languages were words of affirmation and physical touch (although now that I'm a mother, they've evolved into words of affirmation and acts of service).

Regardless of whether you take the test yourself or whether you find Chapman's framework helpful, this week's devotion is about how to interpret the signs that your significant other is trying their best to show you love, and how you in turn can show them love in the way that's most meaningful to them.

In what areas might your partner be trying to show you love that you may not realize? Are you getting frustrated by trying to show them love in ways they might not recognize? Once you've determined how your significant other feels and shows love, it's important to pay attention. It can be easy to forget that your significant other may be showing love in a way that's different from how you typically feel loved.

If you do something that your significant other seems to really appreciate, do it again—and then think of ways you can expand on that. If your significant other feels love when you're just spending time with them, make an effort to set aside time for simply being with them. If they feel love through words of affirmation, try to make a habit of writing notes or sending encouraging texts from time to time. What might feel like small but intentional changes will let you reap the benefit of a happy and fulfilled significant other, and who doesn't want that?

Lastly, if you feel your significant other isn't really speaking your love language (whether you're using Chapman's definitions or not), try having an honest conversation about what makes you feel loved. Then, if your partner does make an effort to speak your love language, be sure to recognize it, remember it, and thank them for it.

WEEK 26: THE COMPARISON TRAP

Hebrews 13:5

"Keep your life free from love of money, and be content with what you have, for he has said, "I will never leave you nor forsake you.""

When you're sitting in a doctor's office or riding in the passenger seat of a car, what are you doing? I would be willing to bet my next Starbucks coffee that you're scrolling through your phone, probably on a social media app. I do it, too. If I were to add up the minutes I spend scrolling through social media, it would probably equal a substantial portion of my day. And the worst part is that I spend so much of that time comparing myself to others.

My social media platform of choice is typically Instagram, where I scroll through pictures of women with cleaner homes who travel the world in fabulous clothes. This can go for romantic relationships, too; it can be easy to see perfectly staged photos of another couple's glamorous date night and feel like your relationship, with all its imperfections, can't compete. Of course, comparison doesn't take place only as we scroll through social media. It can happen anywhere, even in our own churches. Have you ever been jealous of the person who always seemed to have a more cheerful attitude than you? Or the person who was asked to lead the Bible study instead of you?

Comparison isn't a one-way street. How often do we post something on social media that portrays our life as some sort of picturesque walk through the park? Do we ever secretly hope that people feel a tinge of jealousy as they hit the Like button? And what for? Often, when we post something that represents a more ideal or polished version of our lives, we're doing so to feel validated or accepted by people we likely don't even know or interact with. But in caring enough about what others think or becoming jealous when we realize we don't have what someone else has, we are showing that our treasure is not stored up in heaven, but here on earth. And, as Jesus says in Matthew 6:21 (NIV), "Where your treasure is, there your heart will be also."

In my experience, the more freely we give of ourselves, our resources, and our time, and the more open our hearts are to loving others, the less we compare ourselves with others. If I see someone on social media, wonder where they are in their relationship with Christ, and feel compassion for them, my notion that they might have a nicer home than I do becomes irrelevant. How much less likely would we be to show off the highlights of our lives on social media if we remembered that many others are struggling through their own circumstances? Why would we try to compare someone else's marriage or dating relationship to ours, when we could instead focus on a deeper understanding of and gratitude for the relationship God has given us?

What we need to understand is that we have the ability to use our relationships, including the ones we maintain through social media, to form like-minded communities in which people build each other up. When we compare our lives to those of friends or strangers, we have to remember that what we see and what people tell us will never be the full story—you never know what someone may be dealing with in secret or be too embarrassed to share. More importantly, God gave us our lives, our circumstances, and our individual stories for a purpose. Remember that your specific story can reach people in a way that others can't. You can use your story to point people to Christ in a way that no one else can! Be thankful for the story you're living. Use it to build up the people around you and encourage them in their faith.

WEEK 27: OPEN AND HONEST DISCUSSIONS

Proverbs 12:22

"Lying lips are an abomination to the Lord, but those who act faithfully are his delight."

After you identify what exactly you have recently fought about, you need to agree on something else: what your most significant disagreement is about. This will be an issue that comes up again and again and doesn't seem to go away.

It comes up in the morning, and it comes up at night. It is the disagreement that you are the most likely to have in public because it is so emotionally charged that you can't control yourself on the issue.

You already trained yourselves to focus on one disagreement at a time with the last exercise. This will be tremendously helpful when you try to get to the heart of what your most common disagreements are about.

As usual, you need to be careful not to try to psychoanalyze yourselves and each other. Your only goal is to go through what disagreements you have and determine which ones are the most common ones.

These should not be too hard to identify. They will be the first disagreements that pop into your mind; write these down in your journals individually and then come together to see if you agree.

It's hard to talk through things rationally because you're emotionally invested in the debate. But you have to remember that your spouse cares, too. Your own feelings are not the only ones you should account for.

No one likes to fight. Both of you wished that you never fought or argued. It is easier to make promises that you will keep your emotions under control than it is actually to control them. Throughout the workbook, you will find countless methods to make this happen.

The first piece of advice I have for you to achieve this goal is the following: it is not always about you. Always prioritizing your own feelings over your partner's is not how you will get to some resolution with them. If you make a habit of considering their feelings more, you will learn to be more empathetic.

You will realize how much your own strong negative emotions stem from wanting to defend yourself instead of watching out for your spouse's feelings.

232

It will be vital for you to work on this skill so you can properly answer this question: what are your biggest disagreements?

Answering this question can potentially tread into some dangerous territory because you are less focused on one topic. As you know, the key to dialectical behavior therapy is staying focused on one issue at a time.

But inevitably, you will have to broaden slightly so you can confront the core problems. Please do not take this as permission to devolve into chaotic arguments with your spouse that does not lead anywhere fruitful.

All of this is only to say, the broader the subject of conversation becomes, and the easier it is to go off the rails into a non-productive conversation. Even with a broader topic like this question, the key is to focus on answering this specific question and nothing else.

One of the saddest feelings in life is to know that a person feels unloved or undervalued. We don't want to feel that way about ourselves. All it takes is for someone to offer support for us to open up to others. But it's hard to know when it's going to happen, and you have to take the lead. You have to take the lead in loving yourself first.

Whether that's because you can't have what you want or you're afraid of getting hurt, you can't control anyone else's choices. But you can control your own reactions, and recognizing that it's always on you to control them.

There will inevitably be emotions that get in the way of a productive discussion, and you should expect this. But you can both still make an effort to push emotions aside as much as you can. The trick to it is having the shared goal of figuring out what your main disagreements are.

Imagine that you are therapists looking at your relationship from the outside, except you were able to watch the two of you in all your private conversations and all the things you said.

Looking at it from this perspective will help you problem-solve instead of getting wrapped up in your emotions and petty arguments. You are better off trying to examine your relationship issues from as objective a point of view as you can.

WEEK 28: SACRED ROLES TO PLAY

Romans 5:5

"And hope does not put us to shame, because God's love has been poured into our hearts through the Holy Spirit who has been given to us."

God's plan for a husband and a wife to work side by side is a plan of teamwork. As this week's scripture suggests, two are better than one. We each have a different part to play, and sacred roles and responsibilities that are uniquely ours, but never forget that you are working as a team for a greater good.

How do you do that? Here are some tips.

Constantly evaluate roles and responsibilities. Each couple's dynamic is different, and each season of life may require you to reevaluate and/or reassign the various roles that each of you play. We encourage you to regularly meet as companions to review your responsibilities and how you're fulfilling them.

Is one spouse trying to carry too heavy a load? Are there ways you can support each other more fully? Some couples never talk about these things and simply expect their spouses to do what they saw their parents do. We don't believe that's the best strategy. If you don't talk about your expectations for how a home will function, then you will run into trouble. Prayerfully consider your current duties, and pay attention to the answers that come. Have the courage to adapt, be flexible, and try new ways of doing things. Workings together as a team includes a special interdependence between spouses that builds trust and makes love grow. By evaluating roles and responsibilities together from time to time, you'll be able to enjoy this interdependence regardless of the season of life you find yourself in.

Play your part with joy. No matter what your roles and responsibilities are, your spouse needs you to choose to play your part with joy. It's too easy to wish you didn't have to do the prosaic tasks before you or to wish you could do what your spouse does or what your friend's spouse does. When you recognize how important it is to fill your current role in your marriage/family, and when you see value in what you can offer and bring to that role, you'll be able to play your part with contentment and optimism. Often the joy of marriage comes in the normal, everyday experiences of sharing life with someone. As you try to find meaning in your roles and responsibilities, you'll find that the mundane realities of life can often be sacred experiences that give you the opportunity to turn outward, show love, and serve the people who matter most to you.

Look for ways to support and help each other. Above all, what matters is how you love and support each other in the roles you play. You are equal partners, after all. Be observant and look for ways to bolster your spouse every day. Ask how they're doing, what they might need help with, and how you can share their load. That doesn't mean you always have to be right there working alongside them, but it does mean that you value your spouse's contributions to your family and life together. Express gratitude often. As you show respect and appreciation for the sacred roles your spouse performs each day (and they do the same for you), the power of your teamwork will manifest itself in new and beautiful ways. You'll both begin to recognize that together you can accomplish and become far more than you ever could on your own.

As you and your spouse choose to value each other and respect your current roles and responsibilities, you'll be able to work together in greater harmony and love, and find joy and meaning in the individualized roles you each have to play. You will find that two are better than one, as the scripture says, and that working as a team is the key to creating the cohesive marriage you've always wanted.

WEEK 29: HANDLING FRUSTRATION IN MARRIAGE

Psalm 34:18

"The Lord is near to the brokenhearted and saves the crushed in spirit."

Welcome to the world of frustration—marriage. You have probably experienced some frustration already; but just wait until you start planning the details of the wedding. Then you can relax—or can you? Frustrations will occur more than you realize once you are married; and some of them will flare into anger.

236

What culprits create frustration? One will be your expectations. We all have expectations, but some have more than others have. You have expectations for yourself, your friends, and your soon-to-be partner and now for your marriage relationship. One problem: Too many expectations remain unspoken. When this happens, expectations may turn into demands.

You cannot expect your partner to read your mind and just "know" what you expect. You cannot expect your partner to be exactly like an idolized parent, or totally unlike the parent. You may expect your partner to supply all you missed as a child. This puts pressure on your partner and will only result in one thing—frustration.

Another cause for frustration is a belief or value from the baby boomer generation—it is called "entitlement." This belief says if you want something, the other person has no right to say no. It confuses desire with obligation. Unfortunately, this mind-set says your partner must give up his or her boundaries for you. It is another form of demanding. This attitude shows little care or concern for a partner. What happens when your partner brings the same attitude into the marriage? The result may be a standoff, a clash, a power struggle and frustration. An attitude of entitlement is doomed to failure; not only won't it work, but it is also contrary to the teaching of Scripture.

Another reason for frustration developing in marriage is the belief that life must be fair. Relationships must be fair and my partner must be fair according to my standard of fairness.

Who determines what is fair? Who said life is fair? If you want to be frustrated, hold on to this belief. It will get you there fast! Keep in mind that frustration doesn't remain frustration; it evolves into anger. Sometimes your anger emerges because you want a better, closer, more intimate relationship with your partner. That's okay, but remembers— responding in frustration and anger won't draw you closer, but will create a greater distance between you. After all, who wants to come close to a frustrated angry partner?

What can you do to keep the frustration out of your marriage? Identify your expectations, evaluate them and discuss them. Evict the feelings of entitlement in your life. Who wants to keep a belief that is doomed to failure? Do the same with the belief that life must be fair.

Then, internalize the guidelines from God's Word. God has preserved those Scriptures through the centuries for a major reason: His guidelines for life are the best because they work.

WEEK 30: BUILD YOUR MARRIAGE ON THE POSITIVES

Romans 12:19

"Beloved, never avenge yourselves, but leave it to the wrath of God, for it is written, "Vengeance is mine, I will repay, says the Lord."

Fact: Couples who have five times as many positives in their marriages as negatives have stable marriages. If that is the case, what can you do to make sure that positives abound in your marriage? Check the following ideas:

Shared Interests. It's important to share interest in your partner as a person, to discover what he/she has experienced during the day, to uncover any upset feelings. This can involve listening and looking at each other—without glancing at the TV or the paper on your lap. It can mean listening without attempting to fix a problem unless asked to do so.

Showing Affection. Being consistently affectionate—and not just at those times when one is interested in sex—is a highly valued positive response. Sometimes nothing is shared verbally. It can be sitting side by side and touching gently or moving close enough that you barely touch while you watch the sun dipping over a mountain with reddish clouds capturing your attention. It could be reaching out and holding hands in public. It can be doing something thoughtful, unrequested and noticed only by your partner.

Perhaps you're in the store and you see a favorite food your spouse enjoys and you buy it for him or her even if you hate it. Or you decide to stop at the store for an item and you call your spouse at home or at work to see if there's anything he or she wants or needs. You are "other" thinking rather than "self" thinking. You follow through with the scriptural teaching in Ephesians 4:32 (NIV), "Be kind and compassionate to one another."

An act of caring can be a phone call to ask if your partner has a prayer request. Acts of caring can mean remembering special dates and anniversaries without being reminded.

Showing Appreciation and Empathy. Another positive is being appreciative. This means going out of your way to notice all the little positive things your partner does and letting him or her know you appreciate them. It also means focusing on the positive experiences and dwelling upon those rather than the negative. Working toward agreement and appreciating the other's perspective is important. Compliments convey appreciation, but they need to be balanced between what persons do and who they are.

Affirmations based on personal qualities are rare, but highly appreciated.

I'm sure you've heard the word empathy time and time again.

Empathy includes rapport—knowing how your spouse would feel in most situations without him or her having to explain. You'll experience something together at the same time through the eyes of your partner.

The Lighter Side. Having a sense of humor and being able to laugh, joke, and have fun gives balance to the serious side of marriage. Some of what you laugh at will be private, and some will be shared with others. Having a sense of humor means you are able to laugh at yourself (even if it sometimes takes a while!), and the two of you can laugh together. Sometimes the best memories are some of those hilarious incidents that happen even though your partner didn't think it was so funny at the time.

WEEK 31: MARRIAGE IS HOLY, TREAT IT AS SUCH

Ephesians 5:25

"Husbands, love your wives, as Christ loved the church and gave himself up for her,"

Couples rarely understand how seriously God takes marriage. Take a moment and think of what it took for some of the greatest men in the Bible to gain favor from God. A lifetime of commitment to salvation and constantly seeking Holiness.

Yet, in his word he says, that he who finds a good wife obtains favor from God. Eternal life and salvation are all free. But God does not make them as easy as reach out and grab. You have to work. Marriage is one of the ways but only when it is done right.

To make sure that you're not confused in the process, God has set rules that should drive any marriage that is pleasing in his eyes. One of these is that you shall not divorce unless in cases of adultery.

He proceeds to emphasis on the importance of love among couples, the qualities of a good wife and a good husband (who should be a provider to his family) and so forth. Each of these factors contributes to making a marriage less challenging and if followed to the letter, it could be a very happy and harmonious life.

Prayer

Lord, we thank you for our marriage and for the far that you have brought us. We thank you today for reminding us of how holy and highly you regard marriage and it is our prayer that every waking day, we will be able to follow your guidelines on having a successful marriage and staying together as that is what makes you happy.

WEEK 32: INTELLECTUAL

James 1:5

"If any of you lacks wisdom, let him ask God, who gives generously to all without reproach, and it will be given him."

As a couple, we feel more connected as we learn and grow together intellectually. How do you keep growing intellectually? Can you recall learning experiences in which you and your partner have felt connected?

We can feel intellectually stimulated when another person shares our same interests. We experience enjoyable moments as we align our thoughts and share insights. Fewer opportunities for conflict exist during these positive engagements. As the joint focus remains on something new and exciting, couples can draw attention to the lighter, peaceful mood.

Especially in a long-term relationship and marriage, seasons may come in which one person seeks to grow skills and knowledge through specific educational pursuits. Changing careers or securing a higher or more satisfying position may be the motivation for this commitment. For whatever reasons a couple decides to pursue intellectual growth, hearing a clear calling to carve a new professional path should benefit the family. Couples can feel connected as they support and encourage each other as they reach their family goals.

It's easier to think of keeping our minds active by learning a trade or sharpening our career skills. Pursuing professional growth is required to remain current and continue adding value to the workforce. Although attending trainings may seem like an individual exercise, we transform a personal activity into a couple connection when we discuss our new insights with our partner.

But learning together can provide even greater opportunities to feel close to each other. Can you consider taking a class or learning a new language together? Perhaps creating time in your schedule to share ideas, opinions and feelings about a topic would help you feel more intellectually connected.

WEEK 33: INTERDEPENDENCE

Galatians 3:28

"There is neither Jew nor Greek, there is neither slave nor free, there is no male and female, for you are all one in Christ Jesus."

Do you find it difficult to depend on someone else? Has anyone ever let you down, harmed or violated your trust? Perhaps the easier question to answer is "How many people have contributed to your difficulty in trusting others?"

Trusting and relying on another imperfect person can leave us feeling uneasy, anxious and even fearful. Speaking the words aloud that we need people can be difficult. It shows vulnerability and may leave us thinking that others will perceive us as weak or inadequate. Even admitting to ourselves that we need others may stir up these thoughts: "What's wrong with me? Why can't I just be strong all by myself? Am I not enough?"

We desire to be enough. And we are! But we were designed to be in relationships. Our Designer planted a longing in our hearts to regularly seek intimacy with him and others. He didn't want us to be alone. Knowing that we can feel more fulfilled and can function better together, we must continue our efforts to work together and maintain a healthy interdependency. With a track record of mutual support and teamwork, we can feel a sense of trust and safety that is matchless.

This helper was not a replica! She came fully equipped with unique perspectives and approaches. God knew that this man needed help! To remember that we exist to help and complement each other is to recognize a vital reason for our design.

WEEK 34: DON'T COMPETE, COORDINATE

Philippians 2:3-4

"Do nothing from rivalry or conceit, but in humility count others more significant than yourselves. Let each of you look not only to his own interests, but also to the interests of others."

In your relationship, you'll find that you and your partner have different strengths and weaknesses. That being the case, you're going to come at various situations with different perspectives and opinions on how to handle them—which, at times, might very well drive you nuts.

Let's say you and your significant other are in the car and having a conversation about a friend who seems to be making bad choices. Let's also say you have the spiritual gift of mercy, while your significant other has the spiritual gift of teaching. You feel your friend really needs someone who will listen to them, understand them, and show sympathy toward their situation—in short, that someone will be able to "love" them into making better choices. On the flip side, your partner feels strongly that your friend needs to be warned that their choices are unwise and confronted about the poor decisions they're making. Once this friend sees how their behavior leads to bad outcomes, they'll have no alternative but to pick a wiser path.

It's clear how the two halves of this couple, with very different spiritual gifts, might butt heads during this conversation. One prefers less confrontation and more compassion. The other prefers a direct "talking to" that clearly outlines how different choices would result in more positive outcomes. Which approach is better?

Sure, while reading a devotional, it's easy to say that all gifts can work together, but in the moment, it might not be so easy to believe. You, with the spiritual gift of mercy, may grumble to yourself (or out loud to your significant other) that their way of handling situations is too confrontational and doesn't show enough compassion. After all, Christ showed compassion all the time to those caught in sin. Your partner, with the spiritual gift of teaching, might point out that if all we ever showed were compassion, no one would ever change for the better. A third person who had the spiritual gift of service might criticize both those approaches, saying we would do better to serve those in need, showing the wayward friend by example the best way to make choices.

What God understands when calling each one of us to Him is that we are all different. We can all look at the same situation and come up with many different ways to handle it, all for the glory of God.

We are encouraged to use the gifts that were given to each of us, and I think that includes validating the gifts of the believers around us as well. You may prefer to teach others a new or better way of doing things, but the gift of mercy may show itself to be more useful in other situations. As much as you may prefer (or even have a tendency to take pride in) your own gifts, do your best to remember the validity and importance of the other gifts God has given to those around you.

If you become frustrated with your significant other's preferred way of handling situations, try to find a common ground where all of your gifts work together for the best possible outcome: the one that honors Christ the most. If two very different people can come together and coordinate their differences for the sake of the Gospel, that is where Christ receives the most glory from us.

If you're unsure about the spiritual gifts you were given, that's okay! Take time to pray and do some research and self-evaluation to see where your tendencies lie. (Of course, if you feel you have the spiritual gift of exhortation, that doesn't necessarily mean you'll never be called to prophecy, just like those with the spiritual gift of teaching will have to hold their tongue and show mercy from time to time.) Once you have a better idea of what your spiritual gifts may be, talk about them with your significant other. Discuss ways you can use your gifts together rather than in competition with each other. Then, going forward, do your best to remember the gifts your partner has been blessed with and allow them to use their specific gifts for the glory of God in coordination with yours.

Romans 12:2

"Do not be conformed to this world, but be transformed by the renewal of your mind, that by testing you may discern what is the will of God, what is good and acceptable and perfect."

After childbearing, couples often spend their years caring for the children, as the necessity for such responsibility demands. Mothers, especially, immersed in her nurturing role and function, tend to neglect her husband unintentionally, of course, to care for her children. Husbands also gets engrossed in his job; the thing that offers the greatest sense of fulfillment, and both lose sight of what their lives together was meant to be.

One way to ensure you keep in tune with each other is to form love habits. Find ways to do little habitual things together that are both meaningful and fun: watching movies, playing a favored game, gardening, exercising, anything that creates a bonding effect. David said: "I delight myself in thy law both day and night." He did it habitually and took pleasure in it. Your devotions can be habits as long as it does not become legalistic. What can you begin to do as a delightful habit this week?

WEEK 36: PARENTING TOGETHER

Proverbs 22:6

"Train up a child in the way he should go; even when he is old, he will not depart from it."

Many children, though planned by God, are never planned by their parents. However, most, if not all, parents do well by their children. Once they become aware that conception has taken place, they begin to make plans for the prenatal and postnatal care of the child or children. Parenting together is an agreement by both parents to sire, love and care for the child together to the best of their ability.

Children demand attention; they need guidance and discipline, love and nurture. To utilize all these components is to have and raise healthy, stable and confident children. Both of you parent together when you make decisions together; decisions to love, decisions to discipline, decisions to plan for the future of your child or children. You don't only make decisions, but you enforce it by keeping them, unless you decide together to alter or change plans accordingly.

You parent together when you decide on discipline and are consistent in enforcing it. You parent together when you model for your child what you want them to be in character and integrity. Your style of parenting might be different, but your agreement must be on par.

Jesus was parented by both His parents. When He went missing, both parents went looking. Both parents were concerned and both parents scolded Him for not being with them. Children need both parents to inculcate the right balance. They need both parents, if they are to be confident in whom they are to become. They need both parents to give them the safety they desire. They need both parents, if they are to be directed to their expected future.

Parenting together may not always be living together, but the policy of joint agreement matters much in the future of their young minds. Decide before conception, decide after conception, decide throughout conception, how you will parent together for the betterment of your children. Children not only live what they learn, but they also learn what they live. So, as our Lord commands: "The things you have learnt, teach them to your children all the time" (See Deuteronomy 6:7) as you parent together.

WEEK 37: LOVING WITHOUT LIMITS

John 3:16

"For God so loved the world, that he gave his only Son, that whoever believes in him should not perish but have eternal life."

As we come to the end of this year, think about these words again: "For God so loved the world..." to the granting of eternal life. Now, let us get philosophical for a moment. What if your love for each other should continuously reflect this eternal concept? What if in everything you do for each other within your marriage, you personified a forever love; a love so unconditional; a love without limits?

God never calls us to do something that is impossible, so you can, can't you? God chose a selfless, sacrificial and costly action by which to portray His love towards us. We owe Him a debt of gratitude we cannot pay because He paid a price He did not owe. Also, as much as we owe Him for dying for us, we owe Him also for keeping us and our marriage together, to see the close of another year.

Start today to thank Him, to think as He thought and do as He did; relaying your lifelong concept of love, not only for another year, but until death do us part.

Colossians 4:5

"Walk in wisdom toward outsiders, making the best use of the time."

One of the best things that you can do to help your marriage out is to spend some more time together. You both need to be willing to invest some time in each other. There are a lot of options of what you are able to do in order to invest your time together. You can learn something new together, laugh together, go on a walk and learn new parts of the town together.

Any time that you can, show your spouse that you are committed to the marriage by making time together a priority. While this can be hard to do, especially with kids, work, and other obligations, it is so important or you and your spouse to actually get a bit of time to work together and enjoy each other's company.

The more time that you are able to spend together as a couple, having some fun, the less time and space is really available for those outside influences to come to cause damage to the marriage. If you are running into troubles with your marriage from the outside influences, then maybe it is time for you and your spouse to spend some more time together, working on your problems, exploring the world, and having some fun in the process.

Matthew 5:8

"Blessed are the pure in heart, for they shall see God."

In your pursuit for happiness even in marriage, you should always remember that your main goal as a Christian and as a child of God is to live a life that pleases the father.

Marriage should not be a reason for you to derail from the path of the greater calling. It is why you have to choose a partner that gives you the urge to continue pursuing Christ with even more vigor. After all, the two of you together should comfort each other in times of difficulty and always be a constant reminder to each other of the love that Christ has for you and the great gift that awaits you if you live your life in accordance to the will of God.

The institution of marriage is pure and holy and after you have tied knot, you vow to keep it as such. You should not let sin creep in or give the devil a chance. With marriage, you have a new challenge which is to not only be the child of God but keep his institution Holy and pure.

The bible has multiple guidelines on keeping your matrimonial bed pure. You should not commit adultery, being faithful and trustworthy and not separating are just some of the few that particular emphasis has been placed upon.

WEEK 40: LAYING THE PERFECT FOUNDATION

Matthew 7:24

"Everyone then who hears these words of mine and does them will be like a wise man who built his house on the rock."

Most of those who have entered into a marriage understand that it is not as picture perfect as what is seen in the movies. It is a lot of hard work. While there are too many people who will enter into the marriage thinking that everything has to be perfect, and then when they and their significant other, end up running into some troubles and falling, they get divorced in a few years.

We all want to make sure that our marriage is forever, not just for a few years. As a couple, you and your spouse want to make sure that your love can last, and that you are not going to become one of the statistics that you hear about in the news all of the time. But while both spouses would love to have all the assurance possible that their marriage will last, there really is no guarantee.

In reality, beyond death and taxes, there isn't really anything that is a guarantee in this life. But there are some principles, that when you apply them can ensure that your marriage is stronger, and that it is able to move in the direction of an unbreakable and long-term commitment.

The first thing to remember is that if you want to have a strong marriage that lasts, God needs to be right there. Everything that you do needs to include God. From praying to asking He for help when times get tough, to centering your relationship on being a Christian, God needs to be part of the marriage. Remember that when you get married, it is not just you and your spouse. It is you, your spouse, and God as part of the marriage. At least that's how it should be if you want to build a strong marriage.

Acts 20:35

"In all things I have shown you that by working hard in this way we must help the weak and remember the words of the Lord Jesus, how he himself said, 'It is more blessed to give than to receive.'"

We often look at generosity as something we'll be able to do at some point in the future. Someday, when life settles down, when we've gained control of our finances and we have more to give, then we'll give more freely. Someday, when we have more time on our hands, then we'll spend more time serving.

But the Bible consistently shows us that generosity is not about the amount of time spent serving or the amount of money we're able to give. Generosity is an attitude of the heart. Generosity is a desire to give, no matter how much we have to begin with. Think of the poor widow in Mark 12 who only gives two copper coins to the church, while many rich people donate much more.

Generosity and giving is also something we should be able to feel, something that makes us trust that God is in control of our finances in the first place. The motives behind our giving make a big impact on how the gift is received by God. The widow in the story above trusted the Lord to provide what she needed, while the rich people gave with the intention of being seen as wealthy or generous. But as Christ points out, He is fully aware of our motives when we give.

The things we save up for and enjoy here on this earth will only be able to make us happy temporarily. By being generous with our earthly gifts, we're saying that our hope is not here on earth, but in our eternal life with Christ. Our life with Christ far surpasses any temporary joy in this life.

What acts of generosity can you and your significant other perform together? If you're starting to talk about marriage and combining finances, how will you build generosity into your budget? If you find yourself struggling to be generous with what you have, remind each other that God does not judge the amount you give. God looks at your heart—where you are putting your hope and what your intentions are in giving.

WEEK 42: THINK BEFORE YOU RESPOND

Philippians 4:8

"Finally, brothers, whatever is true, whatever is honorable, whatever is just, whatever is pure, whatever is lovely, whatever is commendable, if there is any excellence, if there is anything worthy of praise, think about these things."

You can either control your emotion or you can let your emotion control you. When you let your emotions control you, you may lose your temper or you may get frustrated. To make matters worse, you can say hurtful words to your spouse that you may regret later on. Remember that there are two things that you cannot take back – time and the words that you have already said. So, be careful.

There is one powerful technique that you can use to control your response to your spouse – take a deep breath and count to 5. If this is not enough, take another deep breath and count to 5 again. This technique is proven to help you control your emotion and your responses.

Taking a deep breath before you respond has the following benefits:

1. It will ensure that you got the whole message. See, sometimes, we respond without even fully understanding what was said to us. This will lead to misunderstanding. Do not formulate a response while your spouse is talking.

2. Taking a deep breath will ensure that you will formulate a better response. When you heard the whole message, it is easier for you to formulate a more sound, diplomatic and appropriate response. Your response will be clearer.

3. Taking a deep breath before talking will ensure that you will not say anything stupid. If you think before you respond, then you will avoid saying dumb things and words that you will regret later on.

4. Taking a deep breath before responding demonstrates a high level of maturity. Thinking before reacting will help you become a better communicator, listener and a thinker.

5. Taking a deep breath before responding calms you down. When you think before you speak, you will have a calmer and more logical response. You will not be carried away by your emotions.

Thinking before you respond will greatly improve your relationship with your spouse and yes, it can possibly save your marriage.

2 Corinthians 7:1

"Since we have these promises, beloved, let us cleanse ourselves from every defilement of body and spirit, bringing holiness to completion in the fear of God."

Broken promises often lead to broken relationships. If you want your relationship to work, then you have to keep your word. When you keep your word, it is easier for your partner to trust you. If you do not follow through your commitments often, your partner will lose faith in you.

Here are some of the tips that would help you keep your promise:

1. If it is not possible for you to keep your promise, be honest. Tell your partner that you cannot keep your promise and give the reason as to why it is impossible for you to keep it. If you have a good reason, your partner will understand.

2. You have to come clean to your partner if you changed your mind and you decided that you will not keep your promise. If you have a good reason, explain this to your partner. It is best to give a better alternative to your partner. For example, you promised your partner that you will go on a cruise in the Bahamas this summer. However, you changed your mind because you think it is better to save the money for the new house. Be open to your spouse about this and tell your partner that

you cannot keep the promise because you changed your mind.

3. Cliché as this may sound, but do not make promises that you are certain that you cannot keep. Do not promise to do something just to end an argument. When you make a promise, you have to be sincere. If you know that it is impossible to fulfil your promise, then do not commit to it.

4. Do not make a promise if you do not have to. Before you make a promise, ask yourself if this is crucial and essential. If not, do not make that promise.

5. If you already made a promise, do everything in your power to deliver it. You made a commitment to someone and it is important to honor that commitment.

6. Remember that there is no small or big promise. You have to keep your promise no matter how small it is.

When you keep your promises, your partner will trust you more. Your partner will feel that you value him or her. Keeping promises can make a huge difference in your marriage and relationship.

Philippians 4:6-7 ESV / 890 helpful votes Helpful Not Helpful

"Do not be anxious about anything, but in everything by prayer and supplication with thanksgiving let your requests be made known to God. And the peace of God, which surpasses all understanding, will guard your hearts and your minds in Christ Jesus."

Each and every relationship is a little schizophrenic. Every relationship is somewhat schizophrenic. There is a natural tendency to be closer to the person you have some relation with, a desire to come closer by sharing your thoughts, pleasures, dreams, and desires.

At the same time, there is a natural tendency to want to distance himself from him. The desire for independence, vulnerability avoidance, remains free and unburdened.

Both these inclinations are natural and create a healthy twilight and flow when they are finished mature, which helps relationships to mature gradually.

Both powers push and pull build a type of interpersonal dance. No, not a Congo or Macarena side.

This is more like the pairing of skating figures where one moment, hand in hand, man and woman are together and in the next instant are far apart, but linked by a shared rhythm, although they remain connected at the opposite ends of the rink to music guided by the same choreographed routine.

Anxiety can easily spill into our relationships and create the same kind of problem. Some of us are plagued by the fear of being similar to others. These anxieties also centered on feelings of weakness, inadequacy, or the fear of assuming responsibility. The solution to these feelings is very often to find ways to gain emotional distance.

These connections often do not gain momentum. They stumble, lose direction, and ultimately die of a lack of deep respect.

A different kind of anxiety around relationships is the reverse. This insecurity will contribute to one's attachment to others. Your partner, friend, or even your child's freedom can sound frightening.

Such fears often lead one to demand intense attention, affection, and time from a partner. There is a reliance on constant reassurance. The person who receives these requests will quickly be drained. Each attempt to show genuine love and commitment is never enough. It is never enough.

Such relationships break up under pressure.

Anxiety has crush-related capabilities. However, even if a relationship survives this stress, you cannot depend on it to be as complete and fulfilling as anxiety would be out of the picture.

Bear in mind that the kind of anxiety we concentrate on has a specific connection with concerns of commitment and emotional intimacy. This differs from social anxiety, panic, phobia, and other anxiety disorders.

Each of these worries can have a major impact on relations, but none of them are specifically concerned about emotional intimacy. The distinction differentiates how fear is surmounted.

Proverbs 11:13

"Whoever goes about slandering reveals secrets, but he who is trustworthy in spirit keeps a thing covered."

There is a very good reason why spouses are exempt from testifying against each other in most courts of law: to ask them to do so is to dishonor the matrimonial commitment that both should share. In that two-way street of talking and listening that makes up communication, there is an unspoken agreement that what is discussed at home stays at home; that it will not be discussed with the neighbors, with friends, with in-laws, or others.

But there is another element – that of trust, trust that your partner will not engage in activities that will harm either of you, trust that if you must brave danger, it will be for a good cause, trust that in all ways you are always and forever safe with this person your partner – because you are partners, lovers and friends.

Trust is an earned commodity. It is not conferred by a priest's blessing or a legal decree. Hopefully, this element of your marriage was present before the ceremony, but sometimes couples are scarcely more than acquaintances when they tie the knot. Trust is an important part of that "to love and to cherish" part of being married. In a good marriage, it is continually built up through good communication, loving exchanges, shared sorrows as well as triumphs, and generally with both parties doing their best to carry out their share of the workload that goes with maintaining a home and a relationship.

John 14:6 ESV / 3 helpful votes Helpful Not Helpful

"Jesus said to him, "I am the way, and the truth, and the life. No one comes to the Father except through me.""

After a lot of soul searching and prayer, God has directed you to the right partner. You have dated in the right way and introduced yourselves and your intentions towards each other to your parents.

God is a God of order. He loves strategy and organization and works in the same way. Everything has to be systematic and right. Marriage becomes your next big step, big step because, unlike courtship where you still had your freedom and your standalone opinion, after marriage, you become one. It is no longer about you but, about us, your care for your partner and they care about you.

It is important to understand the depth of scripture when it says that you become one flesh. Technically, you're to remain as your individual selves but, your behavior, care and even how you talk is to reflect your better half.

That means that you're not only getting married to your partner but, you're to treat them the same way you would treat yourself. You prioritize them and they do the same for you. This is one of the most vital bible verses that can make your marriage a success. Unfortunately, most couples rarely pay attention to the grave impact that it has if practiced to the letter.

Prayer

Almighty God, you have seen it right in your eyes to bless me with a wife (or husband) and I receive your blessings with my arms wide open. I pray that you will teach me to treat them with compassion, love them unconditionally and through their faults that my marriage will work for the glory of your name.

WEEK 47: EQUALITY OVER INEQUALITY

Romans 2:11

"For God shows no partiality."

You and your partner are different in many things, which are a perfectly normal and healthy thing, while one shouldn't expect their partner to adopt their opinions, beliefs and perception – the only thing you may require is understanding your differences and showing appreciation for these same differences as well as similarities you can note between the two of you. These differences are displayed by adopting different roles in the relationship based on individual abilities and skills that your partner and you have. One of you might be better at resolving conflicts, and one of you may be a better listener, and so on. However, these differences should be appreciated in terms of allowing your partner to use their abilities to help the overall improvement of your relationship and overcoming issues and problems you may have in your relationship. You should both encourage mutual and individual expression and identify as equal when it comes to the way your relationship is functioning. In case one of the partners is visibly dominant in all or majority of aspects of your relationship, chances for conflict and disagreements are consequently increased. Moreover, the less dominant partner may feel the lack of appreciation, validation and recognition due to the other partner's open dominance in majority of aspects in the relationship. This is exactly why you need to practice on implementing equality in your relationship, meaning that both partners should equally participate while making decisions regarding the relationship together and within mutual agreements.

WEEK 48: SET RELATIONSHIP GOALS

Philippians 3:13-14

"Brothers, I do not consider that I have made it my own. But one thing I do: forgetting what lies behind and straining forward to what lies ahead, I press on toward the goal for the prize of the upward call of God in Christ Jesus."

By the time you have arrived to step five as a couple, you have probably realized that you have a strong motivation for working on improving your relationship. In case you have successfully mastered acceptance, appreciation, empathy, connection and intimacy, consciousness and equality exercises, which means that you and your partner have full support for each other while mutually working on the same goal. The strength of your relationship lies in the fact that you have decided to be there for each other and invest some effort in your relationship in order to stay together and enjoy each other's company. Once you have created a joint list of improvements and things you love about your relationship, while also admitting each other what is it you love the most about each other and your relationship, you are ready for setting relationship goals. This practice should take your cooperation and support to the next level, while helping you practice decision making as a couple. Instead of making a list of goals as if it was the case with listing "pros" and "cons" of your relationship within step three, you will be setting goals gradually, deciding together which aspect of your relationship should be improved first. You can set a new goal for each other and together, one by one, at every several weeks. Let's say that you decide to complete a new goal every two weeks, or more if you feel like a certain goal is more complex and should take more time. You should start with smaller goals first then gradually progress to working on completing more difficult and more complex goals. For example, if you and your partner can agree that your relationship feels a bit "stale" as you are used to each other and don't go out anymore or you are stagnating when it comes to passion, you can set a goal to improve the dynamics of your relationship. So, you may agree to go out together once or twice a week to stir things up a bit and retrieve dynamics to your relationship. If you manage to respect the decision for two weeks in a row, the goal is successfully completed; however, you should continue to implement this activity into your relationship even outside the said time frame in order to consider this aspect of your relationship to be improved. After completing simpler goals, you can work towards setting more complex goals. As you are successfully completing goals with lower complexity, you and your partner should gain enough confidence to continue with setting goals and improving your relationship. After simpler goals are completed, you can move onto more complex goals, which should naturally take more time until improvement is noted. For example, a complex goal would be working on conflict resolution without violent behavior, offending and cursing, in case you have this problem in your relationship. For more specific solutions on common problems in relationship.

1 Timothy 6:10

"For the love of money is a root of all kinds of evils. It is through this craving that some have wandered away from the faith and pierced themselves with many pangs."

While not the most romantic thing in the world, money and finances are actually a pain point in many relationships where a couple is married, engaged to be married or living together. As a couple, you share many things, so money and finances and the way the money is spent on everyday basis might also be shared. For instance, if you live together with your partner, you will share your rent or pay the bills together, or agree to share the money you spend on food. You probably have shared finances and personal fund that you spend on your own clothes, coffee, lunch break, etc. Even when finances are not shared, the mere pressure that comes with bills and financial obligations can affect a relationship when there is a case of financial crisis that one or both partners are struggling with. Stress is a common side effect that arrives with money problems, so once the financial problems kick in, the stress levels consequently hit the roof. Especially in cases where finances are shared between a couple, in times of crisis, one or both partners may blame each other, which as a consequence brings more problems to the table and shakes up the foundation of the relationship. It is important to stay strong and figure out what to do, together, especially in times of crisis when cooperation, clear communication, trust and support are all about to be tested. It is in the times of crisis that the strength of a relationship is best tested. What may additionally complicate the case when finances are shared between couples is that one of the partners may be a spender and the other saver. In this case, the couple needs to learn how to take the best from both, while enhancing strengths and addressing weaknesses in the way they dispose with money. Making a plan on how to spend joint finances and sticking to that plan might be the best solution to avoid arguing about finances, while such decisions shouldn't be made in the middle of a conflict. Sharing financial responsibilities when living together is also an important thing to do in order to avoid arguments related to finances and money, so you may decide which part of your money is reserved for personal spending and which part is due to be spent on mutual expenses. Both partners need to take an equal share of responsibility so conflicts can be avoided.

WEEK 50: PHYSICAL INTIMACY

Genesis 2:24

"Therefore, a man shall leave his father and his mother and hold fast to his wife, and they shall become one flesh."

Physical intimacy is the type that most people think of when they hear the term "intimacy," and it is the kind that we will be most concerned within this book, as it is the type of intimacy that includes sex and all activities related to sex. It also involves other non-sexual types of physical contact such as hugging and kissing. Physical intimacy can be found in close friendships or familial relationships where hugging and kisses on the cheek are common, but it is most often found in romantic relationships.

Physical intimacy is the type of intimacy involved when people are trying to make each other orgasm. Physical intimacy is almost always required for orgasm.

It is also possible to be intimate with you, and while this begins with the emotional intimacy of self-awareness, it also involves the physical intimacy of masturbation and physical self-exploration. I define sexual, physical intimacy of the self as being in touch with the parts of yourself physically that you would not normally be in touch with. If you are a woman, your breasts, your clitoris, your vagina and your anus. If you are a man, your testicles, your penis, your anus. Being able to be physically intimate with yourself allows you to have more fulfilling sex, more fulfilling orgasms and a more fulfilling overall relationship with your body. Allowing someone to be physically intimate with you in a sexual way is also an emotionally intimate experience, regardless of your relationship with the person. Being in charge of your own body while it is in the hands of another person is very important and this is why masturbation is such a key element to physical intimacy.

You can think of physical intimacy as something that breaks the barrier of personal space. By this definition, this includes touching of any sort, but especially sexual intercourse, kissing touching, and anything else of a sexual nature. When you are having sex with anyone, regardless of whether you have romantic feelings for them or not, you are having a physically intimate relationship with them. The difference between a relationship that involves physical intimacy alone and no other forms of intimacy and a romantic relationship is that a romantic relationship will also involve emotional intimacy, shared activities and intellectual intimacy is that a deep and lasting romantic relationship will need to include all of these forms of intimacy at once.

James 5:13

"Is anyone among you suffering? Let him pray. Is anyone cheerful? Let him sing praise."

Spending more time together is crucial for perseverance of your relationship; however, having some "me" time also matters. Alone time in strengthening activities for couples? Even though it may appear as odd, this is exactly what both partners need in order to be able to function together. Regardless of how much you love spending time with your partner and regardless of how great it feels when you are together as a couple, both partners would still use some healthy "me" time. In case you are sharing a living space, this activity comes as even more important as it may represent a great way of practicing your individual growth. As well as you are making a commitment to work on your relationship, you should likewise dedicate to your own personal goals and self-improvement. That way, you will be able to give more to your relationship as you are growing as a person and progressing in completing your personal goals. You can have physical and mental "alone time". In the first case, you may isolate yourself for a day or for several hours, as you wish, and dedicate to an activity that matters to you on a personal and individual level. Whether you are working on a project, planting a garden or just relaxing with some of your favorite music, you need to take advantage of your alone time the best way possible. Some people need alone time more often as this is a way they are able to "charge batteries", so don't be confused or offended in case your partner has a greater need to spend some time alone when compared to your need for "me" time. You can freely discuss any doubts or fears that you might have regarding this case. Just be open, honest, and have some trust in your partner.

Now that we have listed some of the top relationship-strengthening activities for couples who are looking for ways to prevent their relationship from going downhill.

WEEK 52: GOD IS ALWAYS WITH US

Matthew 1:23

"Behold, the virgin shall conceive and bear a son, and they shall call his name Immanuel" (which means, God with us).

As you work through this guidebook and learn more about your spouse and your marriage, there are going to be a lot of things to focus on. But the number one thing that you should concentrate your time on is how God is always with you and will always be with you.

Fear is going to be one of the most popular weapons that Satan brings out to use against us. And one of the biggest lies that we are going to hear from Satan is the lie that God is too far away from us, or that He is absent from our presence. And since we have spent some time in this guidebook talking about the importance of God and how you need to invite Him into your marriage, the thought that God is absent from your life and is far away can be really scary.

Has there ever been a time that you felt this kind of fear before? If you have, then you are a part of the club that is going to include most of the people in the world. We all may have gone through a time when we felt that God was too distant from us to care, or maybe we even assumed that He was ignorant of what was going on in our lives because we didn't matter enough to Him.

But the thing to remember here is that these lies couldn't be further from the truth. God promises in the Bible over and over again that He is going to be with us all of the time. In addition to saying the words, God has proven over and over again in the Bible, and even in our modern lives, that he isn't far away, he is actually there.

If God can be there through all of these tough times, then He can be there to help you out in both good and bad times. The best thing that you can do to keep a memory of this is to remember how God's Word promises us of Him always being there and his immense presence in our lives. To help you remember this, there are several scriptures from the Bible that you can turn to any time that you feel like God has abandoned you.

This first verse is a great example of how you can see God present with His people. God commands the people to be strong and courageous and not to lose faith. But it isn't just a command that has no meaning. God takes this further and says that He is going to be right there along with you. He talks about how He will be there through the scary time, the sad times, and the good times, and how He would never leave or forsake His people. And it doesn't matter where you go; God is going to be there still to help you through it.

How wonderful is it to know that we are the people of God! And because of this, because we are believers of God, He promises always to be there and protect us. He promises to be there to help us out and to strengthen us. Why should we be afraid of anything when we know that God is going to be right there behind us?

Think about having to face something scary at school or at work. If you had to face it on your own, then this can be really scary. You may think about not doing it at least a few times. But, then, the biggest kid at school, or one of your managers at work, agrees to stand behind you and to speak up on your behalf during that time. How do you feel when you have that added support behind you to help?

This is the same thing with God. He is not here just to watch us fail. He promises to always be right there behind us, ready to support us and be there through the hard stuff and the good stuff, no matter what. When you feel like things are not going your way, or you are worried about whether you will be able to improve your marriage or not, you can just lean on the help of God.

There are going to be times in your life when you will need to do things in front of other people that may make you scared. And if you have to do these things to prove your faith and to do the work of God, it is natural to be a bit nervous with our society that is really against Christianity and some of the beliefs that come with that kind of religion.

CONCLUSION

Thank you for making it to the end. The next step is to get started with this devotional and see the power that it is able to bring to your life. It is only a few minutes of your week, some quality time for you and your spouse to sit down together, reading a bit of Scripture, learning more about the different situations that are going on in your life and how to handle them, and praying. In these few minutes, you are going to see a big change in your whole life, and it will be for the better.

There is a warped notion of how Christians should portray love and be in love. Unfortunately, most people don't seem to understand this which makes it very hard to be a Christian and be in love in the current world.

You don't have to be part of the confused masses. The truth is, God created man and woman and he created love. Of course, considering how emotions can be misunderstood, he devised ways that would make love not only holy but right. If you're able to follow these ways regardless of the stage you're in as a couple, you're assured of happiness and bliss and above all to be right with your maker.

Committing your relationship and indeed partnership to the Almighty is the right way to finding happiness for couples. Life can be unstable and quarrels can bring down even the best and strong relationships. When that happens, there is only one way to go-the Bible. Find out what God says about love and staying together as two people meant for each other. The Christian love is not the same as the fairy-tale love. Things do not imaginarily fall into place when two people come together to share their lives. It's a journey that is long and tiresome. As a Christian, the best way to ensure the journey is successful is by involving God in it, letting Him be

276

the lead every step of the way. A couple that prays together always stays together. Pray every day that your relationship may benefit each of you and above all glorify God.

In turning to this devotional, you're choosing to notice the celebration by setting a daily, divine appointment with God. If you're the type of person who makes to-do lists, why not put time with this devotional as the first thing on your list each day? There is truly nothing that compares with the soul-nourishment you'll receive from spending even just a few minutes of private time focused on God.

I hope you have learned something!

Made in the USA
Monee, IL
17 November 2021

82354683R00155